James Chancy

Why should Priests wed?

James Chancy

**Why should Priests wed?**

ISBN/EAN: 9783744749435

Printed in Europe, USA, Canada, Australia, Japan

Cover: Foto ©Lupo / pixelio.de

More available books at **www.hansebooks.com**

# WHY SHOULD PRIESTS WED?

By J. C.

"So dear to heaven is saintly chastity
That, where a soul is found sincerely so,
A thousand liveried angels lacky her."

New York:
A. E. COSTELLO.
1888.

# PREFACE.

This book would never, in all probability, have been published, were it not for the recent appearance of an immoral and untruthful work compiled by a Protestant minister, who has plenty of capital at his back to circulate his slanderous brochure. Therefore this task was undertaken, in the cause of truth and morality, and without the slightest suggestion from any ecclesiastic.

The subject of clerical celibacy has been many times handled by priests and laymen who have been as distinguished for their learning as they have been remarkable for their piety. In these pages will be found a clear, concise statement of the case. We have not written the book for controversialists, or for any particular class in the community, but for the public generally. Our object has been to satisfy inquirers who have not the leisure or the opportunity to peruse bulky volumes.

Unlike our opponents, we have given our authorities for every statement we have made, and we have asserted nothing at second hand. Time and again the teachings of the Catholic Church have been reviled and maliciously misrepresented. Charges the most libellous and atrocious have been made againt that divine institution which has been the bulwark of civilization—charges which bring their own refutation, and which no intelligent mind could receive or believe. The main intention of such opponents has been to inflame the people against the Catholic Church, and not to ascertain where error lies or in what consists the truth.

This book appeals to the people. It is written for the people. Our researches have been conducted with patience and sincerity, to bring together all that has been honestly urged against the practices of clerical celibacy and confession, and all that it is necessary to state in favor of those practices for the impartial consideration of the public.

Clerical celibacy and confession have ever been the especial objects of Protestant attacks. But the same amount of talent and the like honesty of purpose have not been exercised in making the attacks as in meeting them. The brightest and keenest intellects of Christendom have cultivated the science of moral theology, bringing to the task years and years of previous study of Holy Scripture, canon law, dogmatic theology, and the whole circle of human knowledge. Thousands and thousands of such commentaries have already appeared, and he would be rash indeed who would insolently style all this great labor "ridiculous study." As to Confession, if the laws of the Church and the exhortations of theologians be observed, nothing can be conceived more conducive to spiritual progress than that Sacrament.

We have largely quoted from Protestant writers to sustain our proposition that clerical celibacy is absolutely necessary to the welfare and purity of any religion. We have given high historical authorities for the fact that all nations in all times have recognized its efficacy. The Russian, the Greek, and the Protestant Churches, by rejecting the practice, have lowered the standard of morality in the countries in which they prevail, and we have proved it by citations from the works of impartial witnesses.

We have regretfully printed the last chapter, because the contemplation of the frailties of human nature is saddening. Our adversaries, however, have challenged us pointedly in this respect, and in answering it we have departed from the rule of our abler predecessors. But it is the truth, and such a terrible array of facts ought to make our enemies forever hold their peace.

In the last published work we have referred to as attacking the Catholic religion through its priestly celibacy and its confessional, the reverend author quotes only a few instances of unchastity, and these are threadbare examples. When a man puts on the clerical garb, he does not at the same time put on infallibility or impeccability. But that garb ought to make him better than other men. We have proven everywhere, but most conclusively in the last chapter, that there is far less to be said against the Catholic priest who is a celibate, than there is against his Protestant ministerial brother who is married.

J. C.

March, 1888.

# CONTENTS.

PREFACE, - - - - - - - - - - iii

## CHAPTER I.

REASON AND RULE, - - - - - - - - - 1
  Specious Protestant Arguments—Sacrifice and Priesthood—Protestantism a mere System of Ethics—Early Popes and Councils.

## CHAPTER II.

OBJECTIONS AND RESPONSES, - - - - - - 10
  Father Perrone's Answers to the Arguments in Favor of a Married Clergy—Scandals that never Existed.

## CHAPTER III.

CHASTITY IN ALL AGES, - - - - - - - 40
  Revered in Pagan as well as in Christian Times—Honors paid to Widowhood—Second Marriages not Favored—Priestly Celibacy Enjoined in every Nation.

## CHAPTER IV.

DIGNITY OF THE PRIESTHOOD, - - - - - - 52
  Count Joseph De Maistre Proves the Practice and Efficacy of Clerical Celibacy—Why there were Married Priests in Apostolic Times—Testimonies from various Sources.

## CHAPTER V.

**CURBING THE PASSIONS,** - - - - - - - 68

Voluntary Austerities among the Manichæans, Buddhists, and Brahmans—Lessons to Protestants—Monasteries and Nunneries—Their Early Establishment and Magnificent Work.

## CHAPTER VI.

**THE CONFESSIONAL,** - - - - - - - 78

Bitter Attacks upon it by Protestants—Ignorant and Fanatical Controversialists—A Divine Institution—Rules of the Church in Confessing Women and Children—The Moral Theology Side of the Question

## CHAPTER VII.

**SCHISMATICAL CHURCHES,** - - - - - - 92

The Greek, Russian, Armenian, Coptic, and others—All have Married Priests and consequently a low Condition of Morals—Mere Puppets of the Government.

## CHAPTER VIII.

**THE RUSSIAN CHURCH,** - - - - - - 102

Its Great Wealth—Divided into Sects—Marriage among its Clergy is a Hindrance to Sanctity and Zeal—Priests Living in Luxury and Despised by the People—Inclined to Protestantism.

## CHAPTER IX.

**HOW PROTESTANTISM "REFORMED",** - - - - 114

Deplorable Effects of Luther's Attacks on Clerical Celibacy—Society in Germany Uprooted—A Frightful Reign of Immorality—What Dr. Döllinger says.

## CHAPTER X.

**THE MARRIED MINISTER,** - - - - - - 128

Contrasted with the Celibate Priest—Christ alone is the Catholic's Spouse—Risks of the Protestant Clergyman—His Follies and his Luxurious Life in England.

## CHAPTER XI

FAMILY, PROPERTY, AND SIMONY, - - - - - 142

A Great Moral Question as it Appears in England—Married Ministers Fly from the Sick—Providing for one's Relatives—Sacking the Monasteries—The Malthusian Theory—The Protestant Church Hated by the Masses.

## CHAPTER XII.

MARRIAGE AND DIVORCE, - - - - - - 153

Laws of the Church and State—Marriage Honored and Revered by Catholics, but lightly Regarded by others—Christ Forbids Divorce—Advice of the Church to those about to Marry.

## CHAPTER XIII.

SENSATIONAL SLANDERS, - - - - - - 176

The Latest and Worst Attacks on Catholic Sacraments—Ridiculous Allegations about the Confessional and Seminaries—A Brilliant List of Converts to Catholicity Refutes the False Charges—Ignorance and Mendacity.

## CHAPTER XIV.

MINISTERS WHO HAVE ERRED, - - - - - 193

"Look on this Picture and on this"—A Partial List of Protestant Clergymen who have given Scandal—An Argument for Clerical Celibacy—Broken Marriage Vows.

# CHAPTER I.

## Reason and Rule.

SPECIOUS PROTESTANT ARGUMENT—SACRIFICE AND PRIESTHOOD—PROTESTANTISM A MERE SYSTEM OF ETHICS—EARLY POPES AND COUNCILS.

Many works have been written against the celibacy of the clergy of the Catholic Church. Most of them are of a scurrilous nature, and the alleged facts they contain have been drawn from the writers' imagination. It is not necessary to notice such literature. Abuse is always a weak argument, nay, it is no argument.

Every now and then a Protestant, with misdirected zeal, denounces clerical celibacy, and rushes into print to prove that it has an immoral tendency, that it is contrary to the spirit of the age and to the natural laws, and has no foundation for its existence in the Bible, and no authority in the primitive Church. There are in every language many refutations of such declarations. In the interests of morality and religion it is necessary, even at this late date, to renew the argument, and to publish the facts upon which the Church founds her clerical celibacy.

PURE SACRIFICE, PURE PRIEST.—The reasons for the observance of continency could be put into a few lines. The exalted character of the Christian priesthood requires that its members should not be trammeled by the ordinary ties of men. Priests, to fulfil the duties of their calling—the care of souls—should not be hampered by the obligation of caring for the bodies of family, relatives, or friends. The idea of the priestly sacrifice is totally opposed to the marriage idea. The purity of the sacrifice demands chastity in the priest. What is there more revolting to the mind, than the idea of a man rising from the embraces of a woman to perform the highest function of religion—the Holy Sacrifice of the Mass?

And here is the point of the whole controversy. If there were no sacrifice in the Catholic religion, there would be no necessity for a priesthood. But there being a sacrifice—the Holy Mass, the essence of the Catholic religion—there must be an agent, the priest, and, as already stated, the purity of that sacrifice imperatively demands that the agent or priest be chaste and pure.

But the Protestant religion rejects the sacrifice and hence the Priesthood. Protestantism is merely a system of ethics. Its ministers are merely gentlemen who meet weekly or oftener a congregation which pays them to deliver essays on morality. In Protestantism there is no absolute necessity for clerical celibacy. The minister has no exclusive and important functions to perform. The Reformers, consequently, threw aside the Sacrament of Holy Order, and whereas the Catholic Church teaches, as an article of faith, a divine distinction between the Clergy and the Laity, Protestants either deny the necessity of any Ordination whatsoever, to enroll one in the ranks of the Ministry, or, if they retain the mere right of the laying on of hands, deny its sacramental character. Hence, there is no Priest in the strict sense;—or, in a vague way, all Christians form part of an unordained Priesthood. This is shown by the practice of business men often taking the place of the recognized ministers, to deliver the weekly homily. According to this system every man may be his own minister—he may work out his own salvation, by merely perusing the Bible and believing in the Saviour.

PROTESTANT MINISTERS AND CATHOLIC PRIESTS.—A Protestant minister may engage in business. There are numerous examples of ministers doing so. The duties of the pastor are few and simple. The duties of the priest are many and exacting. The priest is paid to devote his whole time and attention to the spiritual needs of his flock. He has the sacraments to administer. The Protestant minister has none. Even marriage, with the Protestant, is reduced to a civil contract, and a layman can "tie the knot." But if the priest has a family to attend to, how is he to find time to administer the Sacraments of the Church? Could he conscientiously ignore sickness and distress in his own family, to go out and soothe and relieve the sick and distressed in other families? Could he conscientiously take pay, and not do what he has been paid to do? Still more, Could he consistently attend cases of small pox, cholera, and other contagious diseases in his parish, and sow the seed of infection in his own family? A married priest is open to greater trials and temptations than an unmarried priest. We will show later on how the married priests of eastern churches are without influence, and how morality in the communities in which they live is at the very lowest ebb.

THE GREEK AND LATIN PRIESTHOOD.—It must be said that the celibacy of the clergy did not become an established law in the Church at large until after many a stormy controversy. After a conflict lasting for ages, and at times convulsing Christendom, celibacy became a feature in the Latin Church. The Greek Church still permits the marriage of the lower orders of the clergy; deacons and presbyters retain the wives which they may have previous to ordination, while bishops, being recruited from the ranks of the regular or monastic clergy, are held to their vows, and remain unmarried. This diversity is one of the points of contention between the Greek and Roman Churches. To trace the origin of priestly celibacy, the operation of the causes that promoted it, the vicissitudes of the long battle between the friends and the opposers of the practice, and its effect upon the character and influence of the Church, is a task which requires vast research. The period of the so-called Reformation produced numerous polemical works, Catholic and Protestant, on the subject. Among the most noted writers are Calixt—*De Conjugio Clericorum*—Carové, and the Brothers Theiner (Altenburg, 1828).

The materials for a history of celibacy lie buried in the writings of the Fathers and Schoolmen, in the acts of synods and the decrees of popes and bishops, in the mediæval chronicles, in the civil legislation of all European countries, and in a hundred other obscure mines, which the student must patiently explore.

CELIBACY AND INDEPENDENCE OF THE CHURCH.—Celibacy contributed to the independence of the Church and aided the Sovereign Pontiffs in building up that compact, well-organized hierarchy, which brought so many blessings upon European society in the ages of transition from barbarism to modern civilization.

The law of the western Church forbids persons living in the married state to be ordained, and persons in holy orders to marry. A careful distinction must be made between the principles on which the law of celibacy is based, and the changes which have taken place in the application of the principle.

The reasons which have impelled the Church to impose celibacy upon the clergy are plain, simple, and cogent, and may be summed up thus: first, that they may serve God with less restraint, and with undivided heart; and second, that, being called to the altar, they may embrace the life of continence, which is holier than that of marriage.

BIBLICAL QUOTATIONS.—Protestants are very fond of quoting the Bible against Catholics, with and without provocation, and on all possible and impossible occasions. Well, let them take heed of what St. Paul says on this very subject of celibacy. Let the reader note that, unless otherwise stated, we quote throughout this work the Protestant Bible, King James version. In the seventh chapter of his epistle to the Corinthians he says:—

"But I would have you without carefulness. He that is unmarried careth for the things that belong to the Lord, how he may please the Lord. But he that is married careth for the things that are of the world, how he may please his wife."

Nothing can be plainer than this. Paul's clear eye and pure spirit discerned the superiority of the state of celibacy over the married state. Everywhere he emphasizes the fact that continence is preferable, that men and women serve God better in the unmarried condition. And if it is true of the layman, how much more so is it in the case of the priest, who has a whole parish or diocese for his family? St. Paul was a man of the world. He spoke from experience and not as an enthusiast or a zealot. St. Paul further says:—

"He that giveth his virgin in marriage doeth well, and he that giveth her not doeth better."

St. John's Words.—St. John, in Revelation, chapter xiv., verses 4 and 5, says :—

"These are they which were not defiled with women, for they are virgins. These are they which follow the Lamb withersoever he goeth. These were redeemed from among men, being the first priests unto God and the Lamb. And in their mouth was found no guile, for they are without fault before the throne of God."

What stronger argument can be needed than the words of Our Blessed Lord Himself :—" There are eunuchs who have made themselves eunuchs for the kingdom of heaven's sake. He that can receive it let him receive it." Matt.. xix. 12. This is conclusive that continence is a more holy state than that of marriage.

Christian Antiquity Speaks.—The voice of Christian antiquity is loud and strong, proving that the law of celibacy is no modern one. The Council of Trent, Sess. xxiv., De Matr. can. 10, severely denounces those who deny the superiority of celibacy :—" It is more blessed to remain in virginity or in celibacy than to be joined in marriage." Thus all Catholics are bound to hold that celibacy is the preferable state, and that it is specially desirable for the clergy. But it does not follow from this that the Church is absolutely bound to impose a law of celibacy on her ministers, nor has she, as a matter of fact, always done so.

Unquestionable Purity of the Early Christians.—Protestants assert that the decline and corruption of the Catholic Church began in the fifteenth century only. They admit that she was good and pure before that, and admit as authoritative all her pronouncements. This being so, they must confess that her pronouncements on the celibacy of the clergy are just, reasonable, entitled to recognition as being made at a time when she was all that her Divine Founder intended she should be. For hundreds of years after the voice of St. Paul had been hushed on earth her Popes and her councils followed his teaching on this question. True, there does not seem to have been any Apostolic legislation on the subject, except that it was required of a bishop that he should have been only once married. But yet, in those early times, there existed this very law of celibacy, although it differed from the present Western law in full force. Then, as now, the law had its opponents. There is nothing, good, bad, or indifferent in this world which has not its defenders and opponents. Even that which is manifestly praiseworthy will meet with objectors. Among the objectors to the law of celibacy in those early days was Paphnutius, the Holy Egyptian Bishop.

THE OPINION OF PAPHNUTIUS.—At the Council of Nicæa Paphnutius, it is said by some, opposed the attempt to impose a continent life on the clergy. Paphnutius was a man distinguished, according to the concurrent testimony of historians, for his great love of chastity. His presence at the Council is a disputed point, and the whole story has been called in question by critics. Nevertheless, he admitted, according to ancient tradition, that a cleric must not marry after ordination; this statement is confirmed by the Apostolic Constitutions, vi. 17, which forbid bishops, priests, and deacons to marry, while the 27th (al. 25th,) Apostolic Canon contains the same prohibition. One of the earliest councils, that of Neocæsarea, held between 314–325, we particularly commend to the notice of Protestants. That council threatened a priest who married after ordination with degradation to the lay state. The Council of Ancyra (now Angora), in

364, laid it down that a deacon could marry in one case only—viz., if at his ordination he had stipulated for liberty to do so.

Thus it was the recognized practice of the ancient Church to prohibit the marriage of those already priests, and this discipline is still maintained in the East.

THE CHANGE IN THE WEST.—A change was made in the West by the 33d Canon of Elvira (in 305 or 306). It required bishops, priests, and all who served the altar (positis in ministerio) to be, even if already married, in continence. The Council of Nicæa refused to impose the law on the whole Church, but it prevailed in the West. It was laid down by a Synod of Carthage in 390 by Innocent I., 70 years later, while Jerome against Jovinian declares that a priest who has already offered Sacrifice for the people must always pray, and therefore always abstain from marriage. Leo and Gregory the Great, and the eighth Council of Toledo, in 653, renewed the prohibitions against the marriage of sub-deacons.

So the law stood when Hildebrand, afterwards Gregory VII., began to exercise a decisive influence in the Church. Leo IX., Nicolas II., Alexander II., and Hildebrand himself, when he came to be Pope, issued stringent decrees against priests living in concubinage. They were forbidden to say Mass or even to serve at the altar; they were to be punished with deposition and the faithful were warned not to hear their Mass. So far Gregory only fought against the corruption of the times and it is mere ignorance to represent him as having instituted the law of celibacy. But about this time, a change did occur in the Canon law. A series of synods, from the beginning of the twelfth century, declared the marriage of persons in Holy Orders to be not only unlawful, but invalid. With regard to persons in minor orders, they were allowed for many centuries to serve in the Church while living as married men. From the twelfth century it was laid down that, if they married, they lost the privileges of the clerical state. However, Boniface VIII., in 1300, permitted them to act as clerics, if they had been only once married, and then to a virgin, provided they had the permission of the bishop and wore the clerical habit.

COUNCIL OF TRENT.—The law of Pope Boniface was renewed by the Council of Trent, Sess. xxiii., Cap. 6, De Reform. The same Council, Can. 9, Sess. xxiv., again pronounced the marriage of clerks in holy orders null and void. At present in the West a married man can receive Holy Orders only if his wife fully consents and herself makes a vow of chastity. If the husband is to be consecrated bishop she must enter a religious order.

## CHAPTER II.

### Objections and Responses.

FATHER PERRONE'S ANSWERS TO THE ARGUMENTS IN FAVOR OF A MARRIED CLERGY—SCANDALS THAT NEVER EXISTED.

The learned Father J. Perrone, of the Society of Jesus, in his "Prælectiones Theologicæ," has clearly and cogently set forth the arguments in favor of clerical celibacy and has fairly stated the objections against the custom. He says that the law was founded on the examples of the Apostles and that the practice was universal in apostolic times, and quotes as authorities Tertullian and St. Jerome. Although, he says, in the first years of the Church, celibacy was not recognized, yet it soon became its custom, and priests were forbidden to live with the wives they had married before ordination. He gives as authorities Origen, Eusebius, and Epiphanius. While there was a certain latitude in its eastern churches, yet in the Latin Church bishop, priests, and deacons were bound to observe the law. St. Mark enjoined celibacy upon the clergy of the Alexandrian church; so did the Patriarch of Antioch upon his, and St. Epiphanius made it the custom.

INDISSOLUBILITY OF MARRIAGE.—And here it may be well to remark that the Church has ever and always held the marriage tie to be sacred. The dictum—"Whom God has joined together, let no man put asunder," the Church has never swerved from. Father Perrone thus speaks of the Paphnutius incident:—

"In concilio autem Nicæno agentibus potissimum Sedis Apostolicæ legatis, ut verisimile videtur, propositum erat Ecclesiæ Romanæ disciplinam extendere ad Ecclesiam universalem. Restitit Paphnutius quoad illos tantum qui matrimonio juncti ad sacros ordines presbyteratûs et diaconatûs ascendissent, quoad reliquos vero, qui cœlibes sacris ordinibus iniati essent, servandam censuit antiquam Ecclesiæ traditionem de non ineundis nuptiis. Ex his patet Nicænam synodum Protestantibus minime patrocinari, cum ipsi contendant posse emendatorum suorum exemplum sacris jam ordinibus initiatos inire conjugium, in concilio autem statutum tantum est, conjugia jam contracta ante ordinationem non esse dissolvenda."

[In the Council of Nice, however, where it appears very certain that the delegates of the Apostolic See took an active part, it was proposed to extend the discipline of the Roman Church to the whole Church. Paphnutius objected, in so far as regards priests and deacons who were married and in holy orders. As to the others, he thought that the celibates who were in holy orders ought to observe the ancient tradition of the Church, and not marry. From this it is clear that the Nicene Synod does not favor Protestants in the least who contend that those already in holy orders could be made better by marrying. In this Council, however, it was laid down that a marriage entered into before ordination could not be dissolved.]

"But," says the learned Jesuit, "those priests who had never been married were not permitted to take wives after ordination, and the law was affirmed by an œcumenical council. Although a univeral law of absolute continence was not imposed in the Nicene Synod, yet most of the bishops in their own dioceses enjoined celibacy upon their clergy. St. Eustace, in his patriarchate of Antioch, ordered the law to be observed; so also St. Alexander, while patriarch of Alexandria, enjoined it upon the whole of Egypt, notwithstanding the contrary opinion of Paphnutius, delivered in the Nicene Synod."

COGENT ARGUMENTS.—Father Perrone deals with the arguments for and against clerical celibacy, and even at this late date nothing new can be added to one side or the other. He discusses the subject according to the scholastic method. The authorities he cites are overwhelming in their number and the excellence of their character.

No example, says Father Perrone, could be given in the Latin Church of bishops, priests, and deacons who, with impunity, made use of their marriage rights entered on before ordination, or who married after receiving ordination. "In the Eastern Churches, prior to the establishment in particular dioceses of the law of continence, some examples occur as given by our adversaries, which, however, may be safely passed over, just as others that are subjoined, since they are not pertinent to the question at issue.

As to the special case cited regarding St. Gregory Nazianzene, the Senior, Stilting proves beyond peradventure, by every kind of argument, against Tillemont, that he begot children from St. Nonna only before his consecration to the episcopacy, and that St. Gregory, the Theologian, was his eldest child.

The Synod of Ancyra, now Angora, speaks of those deacons, who, against their will, were forced to take ordination, as happened not unfrequently in that age.

In fine, the Synod of Trulla permitted, contrary to the laws of the greater number, that deacons and priests might lawfully live with the wives they had married before ordination; which action, although a departure from the more rigid discipline, by no manner of means helps the position of Protestants.

SUITABLE TO THE CLERICAL STATE.—Then he goes on to prove that the law of continence imposed on ministers is most suitable to the clerical state.

That law, he argues, must be regarded as by far the most suitable to that condition, which brings with it holiness of life, conduces to the proper performance of sacred duties, and also wards off those impediments which cannot be associated with the methods of ecclesiastical life. Such, in fact, was the law of continence imposed on sacred ministers.

"That the law of continence is holy by reason of its object no one will presume to deny who recalls to mind the fact that continence was repeatedly commended in the strongest terms, both by words and deeds, by Christ Our Saviour, and by the Apostles. Christ sanctified in his own person and recommended it (Matt. xix., 2.) in reply to his apostles, who were astounded at his remarks concerning the marriage state, and said: 'If that be the case of a man with his wife, it is not good to marry.' He said unto them: 'All men cannot receive this saying, save they to whom it is given. There be eunuchs who have made themselves eunuchs for the Kingdom of heaven. He that is able to receive it, let him receive it.' The Apostle (Paul) also confirmed it by his own example, and throughout an entire chapter commended it to others (I. Cor. vii.). The other Apostles observed it, as shown from Tertullian and Jerome. This law, in fact, has its origin in their establishing, and so far as the Latin Church is concerned, it was imposed by the Prince of the Apostles (Peter) himself. Educated in this school, the Fathers of apostolic times and those who followed them all professed continence. Wherefore this institution has prevailed from that age of the Church which Protestants so highly extol.

EXCELS IN HOLINESS AND DIGNITY.—It is no difficult task to show how very suitable this law is to the state of those on whom it is imposed. In its very nature, and by the unanimous consent of the Fathers and of all peoples, as even our adversaries will not deny, it is very clear that this state, to which men are chosen for the work of the Lord, and sacred offices, and in which they are constituted, as it were, the mediators between God and men, far excels all others in holiness and dignity. Now, the sublimer and holier the nature of any state, so much the holier and sublimer manner of life is demanded. Hence it is clearly demonstrated that the condition of such should be that of celibacy, as the examples and institutes of Christ and his Apostles, and the institutes, and sense of all peoples prove.

Besides, it is not less manifest that this law conduces greatly to the proper fulfilment of the duties annexed to the clerical state. The chief offices of the clerical state are to offer sacrifice, pray, supervise, teach, administer the sacraments, care for the infirm and poor, and to perform like duties of religion and charity, which require a man free from distracting cares about other matters, and one who can be the counsellor of all, their judge and father, and even the servant and minister of those whose needs and salvation he is bound to look after. Now who will deny that celibacy conduces more to the performance of such duties than wedded life?

Wherefore, if the Apostle declares that "he who is without a wife careth for the things that belong to the Lord, how he may be pleasing to God, but he who is married careth for the things that are of the world, how he may please his wife, and is thus divided," much less, surely, is the marriage state suitable to the Lord's ministers than celibacy.

CALVIN'S ACKNOWLEDGMENT.—Calvin acknowledged this fact in his commentary on St. Paul's words. "Therefore we must understand," he says, "that the married man is divided, because he devotes himself partly to God and partly to his spouse; he does not belong wholly to God. The sum total of Paul's argument is that celibacy is better than wedlock, because there is greater liberty therein for the service of God."

Add to this that celibacy, rather than wedlock, begets the homage and veneration of the people for the ministers of the Church, and the ministers themselves are better prepared for the administration of the sacraments with assiduity, and for the care of the sick and poor, as daily experience proves. Indeed, the office of a Christian priest carries with it nothing of mortality, but rather exhibits him to men as it were the living image of the divinity. In fine, imagine a priest who is a husband at the same time, and attach to him the name of husband and father, and you have, as it were, pulled him down from his heavenly state, nor can you discover anything in his conduct or life that will distinguish him from other men.

DIFFICULTIES OF THE MARRIED.—"Finally, it is clear," says Perrone, "that those obstacles to the proper discharge of sacerdotal duties which exist in wedded life, are entirely removed from the state of celibacy. For if any one will examine the relative duties of clerics and married men, he will quickly discover the truth of what is said. The married man is hampered with innumerable household economies and cares; he must provide for the support of his wife and children; he must educate his children, and consult for their future lot in life, and shoulder not a few other matrimonial burdens which serve to frighten off great numbers of men from contracting marriage.

"Moreover, if, by the testimony of the Apostle, (II. Tim. ii. 4,) no man being a soldier to God entangleth himself with the affairs of this life—so that he may be freer in the performance of his duties—there is no one who can fail to see that the celibate minister of the Church is free from all these burdens, and that it should be forbidden him to engage in secular affairs, to distribute among his relatives ecclesiastical property, and to constitute hereditary ecclesiastical dignities, to the great detriment of the Church. That which he possesses of his own he can devote to the help of the poor, he can visit those suffering from the plague or other contagious disease, and he may deny himself much, which, if he were married, he could not do. Suppose he were set over a parish in a small village or hamlet, where the poor people could hardly provide for him the necessaries of life? Suppose he desired to bear the light of Christianity to fierce and barbarous peoples? How then?

"If you reflect on these things; if you consider the holiness of the clerical state, and the excellence of its offices, and then recall the grave disadvantages and impediments of wedlock, which the law of celibacy removes, you will surely discover on what just grounds the same law of chastity is imposed on sacred ministers."

OBJECTIONS.—The following are the objections fairly stated against the law:—

"1. The origin of this law is of no help to Catholic

celibates, for the reason that the Apostle recommended continence not *absolutely*, but *because of pressing necessity*, (present distress) as he himself says, or on account of the ruthless persecutions by which it came to pass that, for the three subsequent centuries, there was hardly any one, even a laic, who cared to marry a wife; when these persecutions therefore ceased, that law which rested only on custom, should have also ceased to bind.

"2. Again, as Calvin well notes, men cannot forbid that which the Lord left free to do, especially in this case, as there can be nothing more iniquitous than to interdict marriage and oblige to continence those unfitted for preserving it.

"3. Nor can clerics accept such a law and promise continence, since no one can undertake and promise that which is beyond his power. But such is continence, which is a gift of God, and God has nowhere promised to bestow it on all desiring it.

"4. SCANDALS AND EVILS.—Hence as many scandals and evils have sprung from this law of continence imposed upon the clergy as ever proceeded from any human institution or law.

"5. Had provision been made for clerics through honest wedlock, they could as well, if not better perform their sacerdotal duties.

"6. The first Christians, although joined in marriage, communicated daily, and spent much time in prayer.

"7. Moreover, that division and solicitude, mentioned by the Apostle, does not withdraw one from the love of God, which is properly satisfied through the love of our neighbor, such as a wife is.

"8. As for succoring the poor, experience proves that the laity are far more liberal than the clergy, who, when rich, spend their resources, aye, and even those of the Church, in procuring the best things of earth for themselves, and in enriching their friends and relations.

"9. Certainly, Job and Tobias had each a wife, yet the former was the 'father of the poor,' and the other, out of his poverty, gave to the needy.

RESPONSE OF THE CHURCH.—Perrone replies as follows :

"1. What is here stated by our adversaries is false. The interpretation put on the Apostle's words is wholly gratuitous, and plainly foreign to Paul's mind, who, by 'present distress' means either the inherent difficulties of wedlock, or the troubles of the time, and the shortness of life, as he explains in verse 29, saying : 'The time is short ; it remaineth that those who have wives be as though they had none.' Since this is common to every age, the apostolic counsel and commendation is not to be restricted to the times of persecution, but relates to all time, as the Fathers of the church and the councils have so understood the words.

"Then, too, our adversaries assume that this law was introduced through custom only, whereas, as we have said, it was sanctioned in the Latin Church, by the authority of St. Peter.

"Thirdly, the falsity of the theory of our adversaries is shown from the fact that the examples which they are accustomed to adduce, of married bishops and priests, generally pertain to the very times of persecution, and from the fact that, on the cessation of persecution, the law of continence flourished at its best, even in the eastern churches.

2. THE CHURCH'S LEGISLATIVE POWER.—"All power is given to the Church, for the edification of the faithful, and therefore, also the power of establishing

laws for the good of the Church itself. Calvin himself will not deny that, both by the divine and the natural law, it is allowable to hunt, speculate, and trade, and yet he strongly commends the decrees of the Church, whereby hunting, speculation, and commerce are interdicted to clerics. Therefore, even Calvin assenting, the Church can forbid that to men, which the Lord has left free for them to do. Still, the Church does not forbid marriage to men, but only in the contingency of their desiring to enter the religious state. This is optional to every one, and no one, therefore, is compelled by the Church to practise celibacy except by his own choice. The clergy, knowingly and willingly, obligate themselves to celibacy. Knowing that this is the condition annexed to the ministry, they freely and of their own accord renounce the right to marry."

3. DIVINE GRACE WILL HELP.—" As to the right of clerics to bind themselves to continence, as something beyond their power, that depends entirely upon the help of divine grace. To those properly seeking it God never denies this grace, just as he never suffers us to be tempted above our strength, as the Council of Trent teaches, in the exposition of Paul's passage to the Corinthians. Who can say that that continence is impossible, when Christ and His Apostles recommended and counselled it, and history furnishes us with so many illustrious examples in every age? If marriage must be permitted to the clergy, because continence is beyond their powers, why, for the same reason, should not other marriages be permitted to those who, by reason of the absence or long-continued sickness of their wives, are unable to remain continent?

4. THOSE ALLEGED SCANDALS.—" As for the alleged scandals among the clergy, arising from this law, whilst

we confess, with St. Augustine, that 'every profession has its black sheep,' and that the law is sometimes violated, since the ministers of the Church do not cease to be men, we yet deny that there have been so many or such great scandals as Protestants and libertines delight in alleging. These people imitate Vigilantius and Jovinian, who, according to St. Jerome, 'had no faith in the modesty of any celibate,' and regarded everybody as like themselves. If in times gone by, especially in the middle ages, there were many such scandals, the evil must be attributed to the political constitution of that age, by which men without vocations were received into the clerical state. Many other causes, too tedious to mention, also existed. Still, Voltaire himself acknowledges that laymen, in every age, have been far worse, morally, than the clergy. Finally, we deny that, from the neglect of the law, any argument can be justly drawn against the law itself. The Church has always vindicated her authority against the violators of this law, and striven to correct their abuses and vices. Dare our adversaries impugn the matrimonial state, because the sacred obligations of wedlock have far oftener been shamefully violated?"

5. REPEAL WILL NOT REFORM.—"Repeal the law of continence, and you will still fail to do away with the vices and sins of this nature. Indeed, among those nations where ecclesiastical celibacy is despised, immoralities are more prevalent than are charged against Catholics. There, most of all, may be found the worst morals, the filthiest assortments of vices, unbridled lust in every class of society, and every kind of infamy and crime. It is enough to look to England and the other countries, where the so-called Reformation prevails, to realize of how little use is the restraint which our

adversaries propose to prevent the occurrence of these evils.

6. "That the early Christians would not have communicated and prayed better and more perfectly, had they been celibates, I deny. Whilst we do not say that these and the like are absolutely inconsistent with wedlock, we still maintain that they can be performed much more holily and perfectly by the celibate, or, as St. John Chrysostom says, 'Prayer is rendered more exact through continence.' What is said of prayer may be understood as even far more applicable to other duties. Besides, there is a great disparity between the things done by a layman and the offices of a priest.

7. DIVIDED SOLICITUDE.— "That this divided solicitude does not withdraw one from the love of God may be true as to its substance, but is altogether false as to its perfection. Even Calvin himself acknowledges this, as we have seen.

8. "This may be true of those who live unmindful of their peculiar state and obligations, but is false as to the rest. It will suffice to read the Ecclesiastical Calendar for one to know that in every age there have been in the Church of God innumerable saintly clerics, who have not only sacrificed all their possessions, but even themselves, for the sake of their neighbor, and the poor especially. Passing over the examples of ancient times, let our adversaries read the lives of St. Charles Borromeo, St. Francis de Sales, the Venerable Bellarmine, and St. Alphonsus Liguori, and let them blush for shame.

9. "If married ecclesiastics were so many Jobs and Tobiases this argument might pass, but experience proves the contrary. The liberality of Anglican prelates is known, but if it be compared with the true liberality and hospitality of the monks and the former Catholic

clergy of England, we shall discover that the Jobs and Tobiases are to be found almost exclusively among the celibate clergy.

OBJECTION.—" The Mosaic priesthood and Protestant ministers, although married, properly performed and do perform the duties of their ministry."

REPLY.—" I deny the parity. As to the Jewish priests, the peculiar constitutions of that people required that they should not be celibates. For God had constituted an hereditary priesthood, and in other ways provided for the wellbeing of priests and people. But these causes, which pertained to religion and government, have passed away under the Christian dispensation. Besides, the nature of that carnal law did not carry with it the perfection which is required in the Christian law. Still, continence was required of the Jewish priests, when they had to perform their functions.

THE PROTESTANT MINISTRY.—" As for Protestant ministers, I say that their office is far too petty to be compared with the duties of a Catholic priest. As a rule, the most that they have to do is to talk once a week to the people. Their ministry does not demand that reverence which the Catholic priesthood does. Protestant ministers exercise hardly any authority over their people, as do the Catholic priests. Catholic priests are bound not only to say the divine office daily, but, moreover, must administer the sacraments to the sick and well. They must preach very often, must look after the needs of orphans, and widows, and poor of every kind, and must perform innumerable other duties, from all of which Protestant ministers are exempt."

DIVINE AND NATURAL LAW.—Perrone then lays down the proposition that the law of continence is opposed neither to the divine law nor to the natural law.

His proof is that—the law of continence is not opposed to the divine law, and that proof is easily gathered from the cited examples and exhortations of Christ and the Apostles; also from the examples of so many men, who, from the remotest antiquity, were distinguished in the Catholic Church for their holiness and learning, all of whom were celibates. Such were Clement of Rome, Hermas, Ignatius, Justin, Cyprian, Ambrose, Basil, the Gregories, Jerome, Augustine, and a multitude of others, all of them celibates.

"Surely," he says "no one will dare to speak of these as violators of the divine law. Moreover, these same holy men extolled in the highest manner the profession of continence and virginity, so that the Calvinist Barbeyrac, who was bitterly hostile to the holy Fathers, inveighed against their excessive laudations of this virtue of chastity. Gibbon, too, also a Protestant and an unbeliever, did not hesitate to say that the Fathers made use of excessive, magnificent and altogether too splendid laudations of continence. (Vid. Gibb., chap. 15.)

NOT A NATURAL LAW.—"That the sacred law of continence is not opposd to the natural law is shown from the fact that, if so, there would be some law of nature obligating each and every individual of the human race to enter matrimony.

"But no such law exists:—1. Because in that event each and every one, male or female, poor or rich, hale or infirm, whether equal to the matrimonial requirements or not, slaves or freemen—all, I say, would be obligated by this law to contract marriage, which surely no one will say, nor do our adversaries contend, since it is absurd, and in many cases would be impossible; 2. Because, if such a law existed, the people would know it; legislators, philosophers, and those skilled in the natural law would recognize it. On the contrary, so far from being regarded as violators of the natural law, the professors of sacred continence have been honored and esteemed in every age, as Henry Morin (Histoire Critique du Célibat) learnedly shows was the case among the Egyptians, Indians, Persians, Greeks, and Romans. This indeed has been acknowledged by not a few of our adversaries, who trace the origin of celibacy in the Christian religion from an ideal mysticism which in the beginning of the Christian era prevailed about celibacy and continence.

"Since, therefore, there exists no law of nature obligating to marriage, we justly conclude that the law of continence imposed on sacred ministers is by no means opposed to the natural law."

OBJECTIONS.—1. Against the first part of the proposition: 1. God commanded all to marry, Genesis i., 28; 2. Words of Christ in Matthew's Gospel, xix., 4; 3. St. Paul to the Hebrews, xiii., 4; 4. Same Apostle in 1st Ep. to Timothy, iv., 1; 5. Also in 1st Corinthians, vii., 2; 6. Same ch., verse 9; 7. See also 1st Timothy, iii., 2, and Ep. to Titus, i., 6; 8. The clear words of Paul in 1st Timothy, v., 14.

RESPONSE.—1. The text of Genesis signifies rather a blessing and fecundity imparted to men. After creating the great whales, etc., God blessed them in like manner, saying: "Increase and multiply, etc." I hardly think our adversaries wish to explain these words as referring to the obligation of marrying. Why, therefore, do they refuse to understand in like manner what is said of the fecundity which they offer as an objection to us?

THE WORDS OF CHRIST AND HIS APOSTLES.—" But granting that it is not a blessing but a command, is this precept to continue for all time, and to affect every single individual of the human species? This is what they never prove. On the contrary, it is clear from the words 'replenish the earth,' that the precept regarded the beginning or the restoration of the human race, which ceases after sufficient propagation; otherwise, neither Christ nor the Apostles would have given the counsel of continence.

"2. Christ here speaks of the indissolubility of marriage already contracted, not of marriage to be contracted.

"3. The Apostle here speaks of those who are married, and exhorts them to preserve their wedded life and marriage bed honorable and undefiled, because, he immediately adds, 'whoremongers and adulterers, God will judge.'

HERETICS WOULD CONDEMN MARRIAGE.—"4. This means that there would arise heretics who would condemn marriage as evil in itself, and coming from the evil principle; such as in fact were Ebionites, Marcionites, Manichæans, and others, all of whom were condemned as heretics by the Church. By no manner of means can it mean the Church, which Paul himself terms the pillar and ground of truth, which declared that marriage was good, and only enjoined celibacy on those who become priests, as something better and more suitable to their state of life.

"5. Means that every one should possess the wife whom he *married*, not whom he should marry, as is evident from the context.

'6. 'It is bettter to marry than to burn'—that is, than to commit fornication. He does not burn who suffers temptation, but by resisting manfully and overcoming it he is rather crowned. The Apostle speaks concerning those who are free, but not concerning those who, for the overcoming of temptation, must have recourse, not to marriage, but to prayer, fasting, watchfulness over the senses, and disciplining of the body, all of which helps and remedies our adversaries abhor as worse than dog or snake.

QUALIFICATIONS FOR THE EPISCOPATE.—" 7. The Apostle says that a bishop should not be a bigamist, but not that he should be married. Otherwise, neither Timothy (to whom he writes) nor the Apostle himself could have been qualified for the episcopate. All antiquity thus understood the words of the Apostle.

"8. This is the meaning of the Apostle:—' I wish, that is, I prefer, that young widows and fornicators should marry and be mothers of families, rather than to live unchastely,' not that he would command them all to marry and forbid them to remain widows. But what has this to do with ecclesiastical celibacy?"

SECOND OBJECTION.—Against the other part of the proposition. Celibacy is opposed to marriage, which is commanded to all by the law of nature, therefore its (celibacy's) profession is opposed to the natural law. (1) Man is inclined by nature to marriage, (2) and to that end the difference in the sexes is ordered by nature. (3) The ancient philosophers taught this on these grounds: (*a*) Nature implants in man the desire of immortality, which man can only satisfy by the reproduction of himself in the begetting of children, in whom the father continues to live. (*b*) It is just the same thing not to give existence to an individual, when it can be done, as to take away the life of an individual already born — which is a most grave crime. (*c*) Every one must restore to nature what he has received from her; but nature has given existence to every individual; therefore, every one must restore to nature, when he is able, this existence by the procreation of another. Hence they always regarded the celibate as guilty of a grave infamy, and judged that he would be punished grievously in the after life, and they looked upon the childless husband as unfortunate.

Response.—"1. Nature may incline a man to marriage, without, however, inducing any obligation to enter that state.

"2. The diversity of sexes *enables* one to marry if he wishes, but it does not put an obligation to marry on all. It is one thing to speak about the natural fitness of things, and another about the natural obligation.

"3. Some philosophers so thought, but on foolish principles.

*a*) "That does not show that the desire of immortality was implanted by nature. Such a desire affects the *individual* and cannot be satisfied by the life of his children, in whom only improperly can the father be said to live.

*b*) The Born and Unborn.— "There is a wide disparity between him who is born, and him who has not yet begun to live. The one who is born has acquired a right to the conservation of his life, which none can destroy without being guilty of grave crime. On the contrary, one not born has neither acquired this right nor can he acquire it, since as yet he does not exist.

*c*) "The obligation of returning to nature that which is received can be only subject to the conditions of its reception. But since a father has given existence to his son, unbound by any obligation, neither is the son obligated to give this existence to another. False and foolish, therefore, are the principles which actuated the old philosophers."

The objection is pressed and discussed as follows:—

"From physiology and medicine.

"1. The instinct by which we are impelled towards matrimony is altogether *irresistible* or invincible.

"2. Hence celibates are peculiarly subject to many diseases of the body and (3) of the mind.

Response.—"I deny the first point—since the almost innumerable number of celibates of both sexes, who, even by the acknowledgment of our adversaries themselves, preserved an undefiled chastity, proves the falsity of the assertion. Nor forget that God assists by his grace those who sincerely pray for his help; only an atheist or materialist will deny God's conduct towards his creatures. If the argument of our adversaries were true, then the governments that favored religious celibacy were taking up the cause of so many hypocrites, and every license should be allowed to those who either cannot marry or who cannot make full use of lawful marriage. But who can bear principles so absurd and proceeding from unbridled lust alone?

Physiologists and Physicians Agree.—"2. I deny the second point—for the reason that the most celebrated physiologists and physicians, who have thoroughly studied the matter, show the contrary to be the case, and further, because daily experience argues the falsity of the assertion. Very many celibates have lived to extreme old age in the best of health. Statistics show that longevity is peculiar to monks and religious—that is, to celibates—as was acknowledged by Bacon, Mahon, Galenus, and many others. Diseases are common to men of every condition and state of life, and not to celibates alone. Medical writers treat of diseases which are peculiar to men of every walk in life, and Hippocrates and many modern physicians have treated of the diseases of married persons, and have shown that that state is far more full of danger than any other.

MENTAL DISORDERS.—"3. As for the mental disorders charged, how do they compare with the distress of mind to which the married are subject? What must not the married man bear, either from a quarrelsome wife, or a crowd of children with angry passions, disobedient, and bad? He must battle with hunger and poverty, so that not a few of his kind repent of their rashness in ever marrying? So far from becoming morose and sad, experience proves that celibates are generally the most jovial and joyous of men. Of course, in a number of celibates, you may find some long-faced, miserable fellows, but that characteristic did not come to them from celibacy, but is natural to them.

Another proposition.—"The law of continence imposed on sacred ministers, instead of being opposed to the well-being of society, on the contrary wonderfully promotes it."

NARROW-MINDED PHILOSOPHERS.—This proposition is directed against those narrow-minded philosophers and politicians who prate about the evils to society arising from ecclesiastical celibacy. These men would take away the liberty of the Catholic clergy, and subject them to the yoke of matrimony.

This is how Perrone argues:—"That law must be said to conduce to the benefit of society and the advantage of the commonwealth, which brings indissolubility to families, and the propagation of the race; which strongly promotes the cultivation of letters and the fine arts; which, in fine, greatly promotes and enlarges the establishments of public beneficence and charity. But such is the law of continence.

DEVOTED TO THE PEOPLE.—"It is, indeed, by that

means (celibacy) that the ministers of the Church, who are public ministers exempt from every domestic concern, can devote themselves wholly to the public advantage and well-being of their brethren and fellow-citizens; whereas, if they were hampered by domestic cares, such as attach to matrimony, they would be little better than shuttle-cocks—compelled to 'hustle' hither and thither in looking after their public and private affairs. Indeed, a married priest would pay more attention to his domestic concerns, than he would to the public weal.

FREED FROM DOMESTIC CARES.—" Priests freed from domestic cares are better fitted for the communication of religious and moral strength to private families, so that married couples may cling to one another with mutual love,—better fitted to consult for their peace, to restrain them from vice and unbridled license and the like, which surely are more hurtful to propagation than all these inconsiderate marriages would seem to favor. Now, as on the strength and consideration of families depend the strength and conservation of society, which is made up of the aggregation of families, a celibate clergy conduces much more to the conservation and perpetuity of society than a married clergy. Again, as the well-being of individuals wholly depends on the well-being and happiness of society, of which they are the members, it is evident that the celibate ministers of the Church cannot promote the welfare of society without at the same time promoting that of every individual.

INTELLECTUAL AND MORAL PHASE.—"As to the intellectual and moral phase of the question, no sane man will deny that one who is wholly devoted to his calling and leads a sublimely excellent life is better able to secure respect and confidence, than one who is mixed up with domestic concerns, and who leads no higher life than those whom he seeks to influence. Such a man is the celibate minister of the Church, who can devote himself entirely, either to the instruction of youth in letters or to training their minds to piety and good conduct. The civic virtues and institution depend on these things, and are so much the more strengthened as the sacred minister is enabled to exercise the greater influence. This religious, intellectual, and moral institution extends also to the fine arts, to science, letters, and the whole life of the freeborn citizen.

"That the institutions of benevolence and charity, in their origin and increase, depend either wholly, or at least in great part, on the celibate life of sacred ministers, the very nature of the subject makes manifest. For they, to whom the crowd of orphans, aged, infirm, and wretched are intrusted, are looked upon in society as the parents and refuge of all, for the especial reason, that they are emancipated from all domestic and public affairs. By their very mode of life, celibate ministers are constituted the mediators between the rich and the poor, between the weak and the powerful, and collect from all sides the means by which they can assist the needy. The rich gives them help and the poor have recourse to them. One can hardly, if at all, conceive such of a married clergy, burthened with wife and offspring.

TRULY PROSPEROUS COUNTRIES.—"Lest any one may suspect that this is all talk, without any warrant practically, it will greatly delight us to confirm every word of it by facts and examples.

"In the first place, it is proven by public statistics that never did a kingdom or province prosper in population and wealth, unless where there were Catholic celibate clergy. If Europe has reached that pinnacle of power and opulence which we behold, we must attribute all of it to so useful an institution. It is enough to notice Italy, France, Belgium, Austria, Catholic Switzerland, Ireland; and if you compare these with the countries in which celibacy is proscribed to the clergy, it will be seen that, other things being equal, they have far greater populations. This can only be ascribed to the celibate life of the Catholic clergy and the power of religion, by which means the laws of marriage are guarded, family ties strengthened, preserved, and increased.

THE TRAINING OF YOUTH.—" What shall I say of the intellectual and religious training of youth, for whose education the celibate Catholic clergy have opened free schools everywhere, so that no class of citizens are denied that instruction which is so necessary in civil society. Compare these literary institutes, which so much conduce to the well-being of society, with the schools of Protestants, and note the immense difference.

Finally, by the indefatigable labors of the Catholic clergy, everywhere may be seen establishments for every class of the unfortunate, and, as the days go by, still more are being erected. See the hospitals, orphan asylums, insane asylums, institutions for the deaf and dumb, and the like.

" With the languishing and falling away of faith, and in civil commotions, have arisen those unbelievers and bitterest enemies of religion and society against the celibacy of Catholics. Yet to this class of men, generally, lawful marriage is abhorrent, because they want to practice at will a celibacy of libertinism. Truly, a new reason offers itself to rulers and real politicians why they should defend so salutary an institution from the foolish invectives of such men, for it is the most fruitful mother and safest nourisher of so many benefits that accrue to society."

Futile Objections.—Let us still further consider the objections against celibacy:—

(1) Celibates defraud the commonwealth of almost innumerable citizens; (2) The trials and disadvantages of celibacy, besides, do no good to any one; (3) to very many, on the other hand, clerical marriages would bring much good, (4) and the clergy themselves would live purer and chaster lives, their children would be well instructed, Zachary and Elizabeth would live again on earth, and their offspring would emulate the virtues of the Precursor. (5) If this institution (law) were universal it would destroy society, and so it cannot be perfection, but only the outcome of an insane and unbalanced mind, and such indeed is the profession of celibacy. (6) The Greek and Roman laws forbade it, and marked celibates with infamy, and subjected them to severe penalties. (7) In fact, Protestant countries prosper whilst Catholic nations are wretched and deserted, so that there can hardly be found enough men to till the ground, or mechanics, or artists, (8) the reason for which is found only in the great multitude of ecclesiastical celibates. (9) Hence the *progressive* spirit of the age no longer tolerates such an institution. (10) And so it has at length come to pass that memorials and petitions have been latterly presented to governments for its abolition, the success of which is hopefully expected.

The real Facts.—This is how Perrone deals with these ten objections:—

1. "It is surprising with what unanimity so-called political economists and Protestants inveigh against ecclesiastical celibacy, as if it were the only ruin of the commonwealth, whilst, at the same time, they ignore that other immense class of celibates who are the true

cause of the evil occurring to nations from celibacy. Besides ecclesiastical celibacy we have the celibacy of the soldier, of the sailor, of the philosopher, of the servant, of the libertine, and if this great class be compared with the few ecclesiastical celibates, it will be seen how ridiculous are the clamors of our adversaries, which are simply the result of their hatred of the Catholic clergy, or rather of the Catholic religion itself. If they are sincere, why don't they strike at the other class of celibates mentioned, by whom a vast human propagation is prevented, and who are the cause of so much unbridled lust and vice? Ecclesiastical celibates, even if they do in some respect defraud the nation of citizens, more than compensate for that, as we have seen.

2. THE REWARD OF VIRTUE.—"The trials and disadvantages of celibacy, if there be any, do this good to the celibate himself—that he will 'obtain the crown'; they do good to all the Christian people, for whom the celibate denies himself; they do good to the orphan, the poor, the sick, in fact, to the whole of society, which derives so much benefit from the celibate, as we have proved.

3. "Exaggerated and chimerical are plainly these alleged advantages from a married clergy, as may be seen in those countries where ecclesiastical celibacy does not exist. For instance, married priests among the Greek Schismatics and in the Empire of Russia are incredibly ignorant, commit simony in the administration of the sacraments, rarely celebrate the divine mysteries, are held in contempt by all, and are only tolerated for political reasons. Among Protestants there is far less respect shown for their married clergy, than is given by Catholics to their priests. English literature

is full of hatred and contempt of the clergy of the Established Church, nor does the stage of the theatre spare them.

4. ANGLICAN CLERGY.—"This fourth objection is fancy, not fact. The same would come to pass among a married clergy, as is common to the married laity. Like causes produce like effects. Thus environment and circumstances would mould their actions. The married Anglican clergy do not show themselves so many Zacharies and Elizabeths, and their children are very far from emulating the virtues of the Baptist. So it is not wedlock that serves as the best remedy for incontinence, but a habit of chastity cultivated from childhood up.

5. "This argument proves too much. If it were a valid one, it would follow that literature and the fine arts should be eliminated also, because, if all devoted themselves to their studies, commerce and agriculture would cease, and all would die of famine.

6. "The Greeks and Romans proscribed and punished the libidinous and vicious celibates, but not those who became such for religion and virtue's sake. This we have shown, and the same is acknowledged by our adversaries, who maintain that the institution of celibacy had its origin, not in the counsels of Christ and the Apostles, but in the ideal perfection and mysticism of the Indians, Greeks, and Romans.

7. ITALIAN CLERGY.—"This seventh proposition is false. Italy alone, which has more clergy than any other country, suffices to prove the falsity of the assertion. This country, in proportion to its area, is more thickly inhabited than China itself. If some other countries are less populous, this is due to other causes, common to Catholic and Protestant countries alike.

8. "The true causes are: The vast emigration to foreign countries, and the difficulties experienced by married people in providing for themselves and families. The fondness for luxurious living is another cause of the decadence in agriculture and the arts. Then, too, licentious living is also a cause of decreasing procreation, and to this add the military life of millions, the celibates in commerce and navigation, travellers, and the many engaged in the arts, who often renounce marriage altogether, or marry only in old age, when they have acquired a competence. Again, the many noble families, where, because of the primogeniture laws, etc., only the eldest marries, and the rest are forced to lead the lives of celibates; the vast number of servants and slaves; the natural disposition of so many men, who couldn't for the life of them stomach the thought of a garrulous wife and a lot of noisy and blubbering children.

9. THE SPIRIT OF LICENSE.—"If by 'spirit of the age' are meant licentious, unbelieving, and riotously-living men, good enough; but not men of wisdom, gravity, and the true political economist. The former have never constituted the 'spirit of the age, but the spirit of license, and they have been despised and abhorred in every age. The spirit of such men is also antagonistic to the Catholic religion. The Church does not regard the spirit of the age, but that of the *ages*. In every age, however, the people have looked with favor on ecclesiastical celibacy. Never have the people desired a married clergy. Should any of their clergy become *bon vivants* or give scandal, the people have asked for their correction or removal from the ministry, and the substitution of better ones, but never have they urged that wives should be provided for them.

10. AN ABSURD PETITION.—"These petitioners and

memorialists for the abolition of celibacy were the few as compared with the many who opposed their designs. Their machinations have always been futile, even among Protestants, and vainly do they flatter themselves about a favorable issue to come. And these libertines never advert to the anomaly of asking the secular government to abrogate an ecclesiastical law, which is of Apostolic institution and has come down to us from the first ages of the Church."

The next difficulty the learned Jesuit sets forth as follows :—" (1) It was this intolerant celibacy which impelled so many members of the regular and secular clergy, in the 16th Century, to bring about the *Reformation*, and which carried with it so much ruin to society ; (2) to which add that celibacy in some measure renders the clergy outside the pale of society. In no way can they be persuaded to defend the laws of society. Hence it comes that this institution, so far from uniting the Church to society, rather estranges and separates it, and in truth makes it a state within a state. And since these celibate clerics acknowledge no bond of allegiance to their country and its soil, they are the more strongly enthralled by a foreign power, namely, the Roman Pontiff. So it comes that, under the color of liberty and independence, the fatherland nourishes in priests so many enemies and traitors, or at least useless citizens, who care nothing for their country's weal and are unfitted for illustrious deeds. Hence the perpetual strifes between the priesthood and the government which afflict society. No matter, therefore, how this law of continence is regarded, it should be eliminated from sound politics."

REFORMATION OR LICENSE.—His answer is complete :—

1. "In the first place, it is false that the regular or secular clergy conceived the idea of the 'Reformation' because of their hatred of celibacy. Other and far different causes are assigned by de Pradt, and he has not a word about celibacy. Henry VIII. was not a celibate, nor did Elizabeth, his daughter, restore the Anglican Reformation on account of celibacy. In fact, both Henry and Elizabeth forbade clerics to marry under severe penalties, and every one knows the story about Cranmer wanting to bring into England the wife whom he had married in Germany. And if those 'reformed' priests, destitute of all shame, conscience, and religion, took advantage of their new position, they were impelled by just the passions and desires by which every day so many married and single libertines give full rein to their licentious dispositions, and were equally disposed to becoming Mahomedans, could they thereby justify their defection."

2. PRIESTS THE FIRST VICTIMS.—" Experience proves that this is all talk, or rather the product of a heated and dreamy imagination. There are no better subjects in a realm, as experience proves, than the ministers of the Catholic Church. They are usually the first victims in civil insurrections. The objections offered are of such a kind as rather to encourage celibacy. The liberty and independence of the Church are in question; otherwise Catholics and Protestants equally would be subjected to the harsh domination of the civil government, amenable to it in dogma, liturgy, and discipline. Take away celibacy, and it would be practically all over with the Church. The conflicting interests and cares of a married priesthood would soon bring about such differences and divisions among them as exist among Protestants.

THE PRIEST UNIVERSAL.—"The Catholic priest is truly 'universal.' He belongs to every age, every country, to the whole world. He participates in the majestic ceremonies of the Metropolitan Cathedral, and he ministers to the spiritual and temporal needs of the heathen and the barbarian. Just as St. Paul 'preached Jesus and him crucified' in so many nations, so does a Francis Xavier traverse the Orient and a Vincent Ferrer the West.

POTENCY OF CATHOLICITY.—"The Catholic religion alone, by its most potent influence on the individual, urges and excites its ministers to great deeds and impresses on them the seal of religion. Protestantism—being of the earth, earthy—stands hesitating between earth and heaven, between Christianity and Hellenism, between rationalism and pantheism. It creeps along the ground, nor can it rise to the conception or performance of any illustrious achievement."

# CHAPTER III.

## Chastity in all Ages.

REVERED IN PAGAN AS WELL AS IN CHRISTIAN TIMES—HONORS PAID TO WIDOWHOOD—SECOND MARRIAGES NOT FAVORED—PRIESTLY CELIBACY ENJOINED IN EVERY NATION.

Chastity in all ages and among all nations has ever exacted respect. The dissolute have paid it involuntary homage. Even in the worst of times men who would not practise it have been forced to admire it. But Protestants have made a great point of the fact that, under the old law, every woman in Israel desired to be married in order to have children. Yet those controversialists have not honestly stated the reason why. The prophecy that the Messiah was to come of the favored race was constantly in the mind of the Jewish maiden. Each hoped that her offspring might be the favored of the Lord. Hence the importance of marriage among the Jews, and the ignominy which attached to barrenness. Nevertheless, widowhood was highly honored. Take the story of Judith, who received the warmest eulogiums because she did not take another husband after the death of Manasses. The people honored her as much for her chastity as for her great victory.

"You are the glory of Jerusalem," said her people, "the joy and honor of our people, for you have great courage, and your heart is strong, because you have loved chastity, and after your husband was dead you would not take another."

WIDOWHOOD HONORED.—Widowhood enjoyed the same honor in Rome as in Greece. Artemisia, praised by the philosophers and poets, was the admiration of all times. The chastity of Penelope, sung by the most sublime of poets, was chanted to the skies. Teuta or Theusa, as Florus calls her, who was queen of Illyria, was considered worthy, on account of her great chastity, to command illustrious warriors, and often defeated the Romans. St. Jerome, who lived so near to the pagan days as to be well acquainted with their customs, tells us that the widows who had not married a second time held a distinguished rank among other women, and that they had the privilege of offering sacrifice to Fortuna. At Rome they had a particular name, *univira*, woman of one husband, a word which is yet found among other titles of honor in epitaphs.

Even in China the same ideas will be found. There widowhood is venerated to such a degree that triumphal arches are erected to preserve the memory of women who remained widows.

OPPOSITION TO SECOND MARRIAGE.—Second marriages have always been looked upon with disfavor in all times. Even in the midst of the deepest corruption of paganism women who desired to preserve their rank, their name, or the honor of their families, did not take a second husband. It is related that Rhodogune, the daughter of Darius, when her nurse advised her to marry again, was so irritated that she killed her on the spot.

Towards the close of the Roman Empire, when manners were so horribly degraded, the hand of Valeria, the widow of Maximian, was sought by the Emperor Maximin. She declined, giving as her reason that it would be contrary to usage and without example that a woman of her name and rank should take a second husband. (Suetonius, *de morte persecut.*, c. xxxix.)

AMONG THE ROMANS.—Portia, a Roman lady, quoted by Hieronymus, said: "a lady who is happy and has a sense of shame would not marry but once."

History and fable alike show that those who were continent were held in esteem by men. Travellers have told that among the Hottentots the woman who marries a second time is obliged to cut off one of her fingers.

The disfavor in which second marriages were held had an injurious effect upon the offspring of the second union. Thus in India the law disinherited the sons of the second marriage.

The following story from Tacitus shows how great was the respect in pagan times paid to continence:— In the time of the Roman emperors, when women like Seneca did not count the years according to the ordinary method, but according to the number of their husbands, two distinguished personages, Pollion and Agrippa, were disputing about the honor of giving a Vestal to the state. "The daughter of Pollion was preferred, because her mother had never taken a second husband, whilst Agrippa had changed his domestic relations by divorce."

St. Paul (I. Cor. vii. 8) says:—"I say therefore to the unmarried and widows, it is good for them if they abide, even as I."

Of the widow he says:—"She is happier if she so abide."—(I. Cor. vii. 40).

Timothy (I. v. 3.) says:—"Honor widows that are widows indeed."

ST. PAUL'S FORESIGHT.—From passages of St. Paul

it is quite clear that the idea of clerical celibacy was already taking root. At the same time, he foresaw how such a law might be abused, and he strongly condemned the heresies which should forbid marriage.

The Fathers of the Church, who are the defenders and depositories of Catholic dogma, have always eulogized widowhood and have exhorted widows to remain in that state. St. Augustine, St. Ambrose, and St. Chrysostom, and others have written treatises upon the subject. The most virtuous women of advanced age were associated with the service of the Church, under the name of deaconesses. True, St. Paul says widows may marry again, if they cannot be continent, but he gives his approval to avoid a great evil. The Fathers of the Church always looked upon second marriages as a mark of incontinence and reluctantly permitted or approved them. Says St. Chrysostom (de non iterando conjug., vol. i., p. 435):—"Signum magnæ cujusdam infirmitatis et socordiæ."

The Council of Neocæsarea, held in 314, forbade priests to assist at banquets given on these occasions.

It it easy to see, when second marriages were disliked by the Apostles and the Fathers, how heartily they must have approved of clerical celibacy.

TESTIMONY OF ANCIENT AUTHORS.—The learned Abbé Jager, writing more than fifty years ago, says that continence attracts the homage of man in the degree in which it approaches perfection. Ancient authors picture the virgin as a superior person, a kind of supernatural being, "worthy," adds the Abbé, "of being *en rapport* with the divinity, of being consecrated to its service." Among all peoples virginity has received the same homage and the same tribute of admiration. What honors were paid to the vestal virgins of Rome and Athens, honors which were reflected on their families! Livy tells us that Numa, to make the Vestals venerated and holy, ordered them to remain virgins. Virgil puts these words into the mouth of Turnus:— "O, decus Italiæ, virgo." (Aen. xi., 508)—"Oh, virgin, the honor of Italy."

In the face of history, in the face of writers of all kinds who have extolled chastity, how monstrous that Luther and his followers of to-day should decry virginity, continence, should assert that it is impossible for men and women to live apart! In India, in China, in Mexico, and in other countries, East and West, virginity has been extolled and honored. The Saviour Himself came from the womb of a Virgin. In the opinion of the Chinese, the saints, the sages, the heroes of the people were born of a virgin. The Gymnosophists, of whom Philostratus speaks, pretended that Buddha, the founder of their religion, was born of a virgin. According to the fable, Plato so came into the world. The Greeks could not conceive that so great a man could have been born of any but a virgin.

THE SENTIMENT OF THE PEOPLE.—"Is this universal testimony in favor of continence lost upon us?" asks the Abbé Jager. "Not by any means. What is in human nature, what is recognized by all, is not lost. Let the Protestants and the philosophers decry at their ease religious celibacy, people will not be the less persuaded that it is above marriage, that it is a holier and more perfect state. Such will be the sentiment of the people, an opinion the more unshaken, because Christianity has strengthened it in all hearts, and has given it an immense impetus. What was formerly astonishing because of its rarity, has become common among us. There are no Vestals to-day, but instead thousands and thousands of virgins, pure as the angels, burning with the devotion of heroism, some consecrating themselves to the education of youth, others to the service of the sick, all to a ministry that may be repugnant or disagreeable.

"Jesus Christ has said :—' And every one that has forsaken home, or brethren, or sisters, or father, or mother, or wife, or children, or lands, for my name's sake, shall receive a hundredfold, and shall inherit everlasting life.' These words have been realized beyond all human expectations.

THE VENGEFUL CRY.—"And they would persuade us that those heroines, those illustrious virgins, the honor of sacerdotal Christianity, the glory of our faith, the consolation of humanity, act contrary to Scripture, violate the rules of the evangels and the natural law! He who would say so, would he not have against him the whole human kind for such a blasphemy, and hear the vengeful cry of indignation for outraged virginity?"

"'Blessed are the pure of heart,' says Christ, 'for they shall see God.'"

PURE WOMEN IN PAGAN TIMES.—In pagan times the women who were pure were honored of all. In Christian times the women who consecrate themselves to a life of chastity are slandered and vilified by impious men. Impious men! Nay, it is men who stand well in the eyes of the world who join in the outrageous cry. From the days of Martin Luther to the present time, the nun has been the object of cowardly attack. No insinuation is too vile to be used against her. Satanic slanders have ever been on the lips of professing Christians. Are their hearts so full of wickedness that they cannot conceive of a woman leading a holy and a chaste life? Think of ladies coming from the proudest families of France, of Spain, of England, of Germany, of Austria, of America, leaving their luxurious homes to lead a life of shame! Great God, the thought is too horrible. The only answer to such vicious and degrading arguments against the Catholic religion is a knock-down blow.

CALUMNY EVERYWHERE.—On the platform, in the press, and even in the pulpit, these villanous diatribes are daily heard or read. And yet the promulgators of such unmistakable falsehoods are received in respectable society, and women do not blush when they hear the name of the vilifiers of their sex mentioned, and do not turn away from the monsters who defame their sisters.

And this is the age of Protestantism!

Monasteries and convents were the products of Christianity. St. Justin, writing in the middle of the second century, said:—"We see in our midst a great number of the faithful of both sexes, who have arrived at the age of sixty or seventy years, having scrupulously preserved their virginity." (St. Just. oper., p. 48, edit 1595.)

HONORING THE VIRGINS.—In the time of St. Cyprian the virgins already formed a distinguished body among the faithful. The Empress Helena thought it an honor to serve with her own hands the virgins at table.

According to St. Chrysostom the city of Antioch contained about 3,000 virgins.

The Third Council of Carthage, held in 597, shows that virgins who had lived in their families after the death of their parents went into a convent for the rest of their days.

St. Jerome observed that in Rome alone the monasteries of the chaste of both sexes were innumerable.

Theodoret, in the middle of the fifth century, adds

his testimony to the infinite number of societies which practised this virtue, not only in his own country, but in the East. Palestine, Egypt, Asia, the whole of Europe, he says, were filled with them.

St. Fulgence says:—" We affirm that virginity is as much above marriage as excellent things are above merely good things, as heavenly things are above worldly things, as an immortal union is above a perishable union, as the spirit is above the flesh."

WHAT PROTESTANTS IGNORE.—Volumes could be filled with such examples. Mosheim, a great Protestant writer, proves, from passages of many Fathers, that the words of Jesus Christ had been taken literally and had inspired the primitive Christians with a great esteem for celibacy. But what Protestants ignore, at least what they have entirely forgotten, is that the vow of chastity has always been regarded as inviolable. To stain it was considered worthy of the severest punishment.

St. Basil says:—" Widowhood being inferior to virginity, what is criminal in widows is still more so in virgins. If widows who have violated their first faith (he means in marrying a second time) are condemned by the Apostle, with much greater reason are virgins who are the spouses of Jesus Christ, and like a vase consecrated to the Lord."

Both St. Basil and St. Chrysostom considered that the fault of a virgin was greater than adultery. The Council of Elvira, held in 305, ordered the excommunication of erring virgins and refused them communion, even at the point of death, unless after their fall they had done penance during the remainder of their life.

PAGANS SHAME THE PROTESTANTS.—Never had been seen before what the leaders of the Reformation permitted after Luther's break from the Church. Even the pagans confound the Protestants by their conduct, for in the punishing of erring virgins they were severer than the Christians. When the vow of chastity had been broken, the punishment that followed was terrible. Minutia, a Roman vestal who was suspected of having broken her promise, was interred alive.

"An unjust penalty," says St. Jerome, "if the violation of virginity had not been in their eyes a great crime." Ancient history gives us many examples of virgins who, sensible of the importance of their promise, suffered death rather than break their vow.

Returning to the Jewish customs, we find that Moses forbade the Levites, under pain of death, to exercise the least of their functions, until they had prepared themselves by the exercise of this virtue of continence. Saith the Lord:—

"Speak unto Aaron and to his sons, that they separate themselves from the holy things of the children of Israel, and that they profane not my holy name in those things which they hallow unto me. I am the Lord. Say unto them, Whosoever he be of all your seed among your generations, that goeth into the holy things which the children of Israel hallow unto the Lord, having his uncleanness upon him, that soul shall be cut off from my presence. I am the Lord. Say unto them, Whosoever he be of all your seed among your generations that goeth unto the holy things which the children of Israel hallow unto the Lord, having his uncleanness upon him, that soul shall be cut off from my presence. I am the Lord."—Lev., xxii. 1, 2, 3.

PRIESTS OF THE OLD LAW.—The longer the duration of the religious function, the more rigorous was the law of continence. The priests of the old law were obliged to live in the Temple, estranged from their wives during the whole year of their ministry. St. Siricius and St. Jerome tell us that the priests returned to their households after their year of service, in order that the tribe of Levi, the priestly race, should not become extinct.

AN IMMENSE MASS OF TESTIMONY.—There is an immense mass of testimony, drawn from every nation, to prove that continence was regarded as indispensable for performing a sacred function. That testimony is incontrovertible. Those priests who assisted at the sacrifice even temporarily were obliged to be continent at least for 24 hours, as we see by the law of Moses and from the testimony of Plutarch.

In Peru there was the *fête* of the new moon in September, after the equinox. It was called the Cancu, and was a religious purification for body and soul, for which preparation was made by the observance of continency. Among the Indians of the New World, the Hurons and the Iroquois, it was considered a crime not to be continent for the 24 hours preceding the ceremony of the "Calumet."

The Hierophant of the Greeks, whose ministrations were for life, was obliged to be continent all his life.

TRUE RELIGION, TRUE VIRGINITY.—St. Alphonsus says that only a true religion can produce true virginity. "Nowhere else but among Christians," said he, "is that holy and heavenly precept of virginity so well fulfilled, and it is one of the greatest proofs that we possess the true religion."

St. Jerome relates (S. Hier. adv. Jov. lib. 2, c. 9.) that the ancient priests of Egypt, renouncing all worldly cares and business, lived in the temples and contemplated the works of nature. From the very moment, he says, that they entered the service of the gods, they abstained from intercourse with women; they lived in continual continence, never drank wine, and devoted themselves to the conquering of every thought of concupiscence.

In the East and in the West the altars of the gods were surrounded by chaste men and by chaste women. No one else had the right of penetrating the sanctuary. The Spartans and the Messenians exchanged virgins for the service of the gods. Among the Persians the obligation of chastity was imposed upon young women destined for the service of the worship of the sun. Among the Gauls nine virgins guarded a famous oracle and were held in great veneration and had special privileges.

OPINION OF THE GREAT GREEK ORATOR.—Demosthenes (contr. Democrat, No. 42) says:—" I am convinced that those who enter the sanctuary, who touch holy things, who preside over Divine worship, ought to be chaste, not alone for a certain period, but during their whole life."

And St. John (Rev. xiv. 4.) speaking of the privileged and the blessed whom he saw around the throne of the Lamb, thus pictures the effect of that holy state which certain fanatical Protestants despise:—" These are they which were not defiled by women, for they are virgins. These are they which follow the Lamb whithersoever he goeth; these were redeemed from among men, being the first fruits unto God and the Lamb."

St. Isidore, speaking of the Apostles, says:—" How could they have guided the souls of the chaste, unless they were so themselves?"—(quo enim pudore viduæ, aut virginis . . . integritatem vel continentiam prædicare.) No, that was not possible, for the priesthood and celibacy were so bound up together in the spirit of Christianity that it was not easy to think of the one without connecting the other with it.

**Sublimity of the Priesthood.**—St. Chrysostom speaks of the sublimity of the Christian priesthood and says that the priest ought to be pure and holy. "It is true," he adds, "that the duties of the priesthood are exercised upon the earth, but, nevertheless, we must accord it a heavenly rank, for this order comes neither from men, nor from angels, nor from any created power. It is the Holy Ghost himself who has established it, and who tells the beings upon earth that it is a heavenly ministry. The priest, then, must be as pure as if he were placed in the midst of the heavenly powers."

St. Ambrose fought with determination the enemies of celibacy. "These breakers of the law of clerical celibacy," said he, "pretend that they have an excuse in the law of Moses. But the priests of that law offered sacrifice only at intervals, and then they washed their clothes and purified themselves for many days previous to offering the sacrifice, as we read in the Old Testament. If the figure demand such preparation, how much more does the reality exact?"

# CHAPTER IV.

## Dignity of the Priesthood.

Count Joseph De Maistre proves the Practice and Efficacy of Clerical Celibacy—Why there were Married Priests in Apostolic Times—Testimonies from various Sources.

One of the weakest arguments offered against clerical celibacy is that in the days immediately after the Apostles and for some time following there were married priests.

There were, truly, but as the Church was in its infancy it could not be otherwise. There were good men and women, even among the Pagans. The wicked and debased do not as readily appreciate virtue and true religion as the good and honest. When these upright married pagans entered the Church of Christ, they became the holiest as well as the most zealous of her children. They became priests. But nowhere does history show that the priests who lost their wives by death married again.

Married Priests Advocate Celibacy.—The preceding chapter gives numerous instances of the esteem in which widowhood was held, even by those who were not Christians. It is not likely that these widowed Christian priests would marry again. In the beginning, when the Church was so small, it was not always easy to find single men who had the virtues, the talent, and the zeal necessary for the priesthood. These qualities were frequently found in the married, and hence they were chosen for the sacred office. But the strongest advocates of clerical celibacy were these very priests who had entered the married state before they had entered the sacerdotal order.

THE VIEWS OF EUSEBIUS.—The observance of clerical celibacy was so noted between 312 and 476 that Eusebius of Cæsarea wrote in his Evangelical Demonstration: "The state of continence is the proper state of those who are devoted to the priesthood and engaged in the ministry of divine worship; of the doctors and the preachers of the divine word, whose care it is to raise a holy and spiritual offspring, and to train to holiness, not a particular family, but the countless multitude of the faithful." The Council of Elvira (33d Canon) decrees that bishops, priests, and deacons, who have entered into the married state before ordination, shall separate entirely from their wives. The Council of Neocæsarea orders that any priest who marries after ordination shall be deposed. The Nicene inveighs against an abuse, which had gained footing in many places, relative to women living under the same roof with clerics, under pretext of ministering to them; they were called in Greek ἀγαπηταί, in Latin *subintroductæ*.

"The Œcumenical Council," says the Canon, "forbids all, whether bishops, priests, deacons, or other clerics, to have under the same roof any woman save a mother, sister, aunt, or other whose relationship precludes all just ground of suspicion."

ANCIENT CUSTOMS.—"It is usual," says the learned Father Thomassin, "to allege against clerical celibacy the story of the holy bishop Paphnutius, who, according to Socrates and Sozomenus, obliged the Fathers of Nice to pass no decree subjecting bishops, priests, and deacons to continence with the wife they had married before ordination, as the ancient tradition only forbade the contraction of new marriages after receiving sacred orders. But the authority of Socrates and Sozomenus is by no means unquestionable. The assertion may be grounded on fact, and Socrates may have erred only in what is his own in the account. But when he says that the *ancient tradition of the Church* only forbade the contraction of marriage ties in the highest orders of the clergy, without depriving them of the use of a preceding marriage, we appeal in this matter to Eusebius, St. Epiphanius, and St. Jerome, who, besides being more ancient than Socrates, were immeasurably better acquainted with the ancient customs of the Church; his assertion, therefore, is unworthy of belief."

DE MAISTRE ON CELIBACY.—Count Joseph De Maistre has gone thoroughly and learnedly into the subject, and of our modern writers his words are among the weightiest. Says the great Frenchman:—

" The whole world has never ceased to bear witness to these great truths : 1st. The eminent merit of chastity, 2d. The natural alliance of continency with all religious functions, but particularly with those of the priesthood.

" Christianity, therefore, in imposing on priests the law of celibacy, has only availed itself of a natural idea : it has disincumbered this idea of all error, given to it a divine sanction, and converted it into a law of the highest discipline. But against this Divine law, human nature was too strong, and could only be overcome by the inflexible and all-conquering power of the Sovereign Pontiff.

" In barbarous ages, above all, nothing less would have sufficed to save the priesthood than the hand of Gregory VII. Without this extraordinary man, all was lost, humanly speaking. The immense power he exercised in his time is complained of; as well might men complain of God Himself, who gave him that strength, without which he could not have acted as he did. The powerful legislator obtained all it was possible to obtain of rebellious elements; and his successors applied to the great work with such perseverance, that they succeeded at last in establishing the priesthood upon immovable foundations.

It Belongs to the Highest Discipline.—" I am far from exaggerating and wishing to speak of the law of celibacy as a dogma, properly so called; but I hold that it belongs to the highest discipline, that it is of unrivalled importance, and that we cannot be too grateful to the Sovereign Pontiff, to whom we are indebted for having maintained it."

De Maistre goes on to prove that the priest who belongs to a wife and children belongs no longer to his flock, or does not sufficiently belong to it. An essential faculty is always wanting to him,—that of giving alms, of exercising charity without sometimes considering too narrowly his own means. In thinking of his children, the married priest dares not follow the impulses of his heart; his purse is tied up against indigence, which has nothing to expect at his hands but cold exhortations. Moreover, the dignity of the priest would be mortally wounded by certain kinds of ridicule. The wife of a superior magistrate, who should manifestly forget her duties, would do more harm to her husband than the wife of any other man. And why? Because the higher magistracies possess a kind of holy and venerable dignity, by which they resemble the priesthood. What would it not be, then, in regard to the priesthood itself?

**Dangers of the Married Priest.**—Not only do the vices of the wife, reflect great discredit on the character of the married priest, but the latter, in his turn, escapes not the danger common to all men engaged in the married state—that of living criminally. The multitude of reasoners who have treated the great question of ecclesiastical celibacy always ground upon the notable sophism that marriage is a state of purity, whilst in reality it is clean only to the clean. How many marriages are irreproachable before God? Infinitely few. The man who is blameless in the eyes of the world may be infamous at the altar. If human weakness or perversity establishes a conventional toleration in regard to certain abuses, this toleration, which is itself an abuse, is never suited to the priest, because the conscience of mankind ceases not to compare it with the type of sacerdotal perfection it contemplates within itself; so that it makes no allowance for the copy, whenever it ceases to be like the pattern.

"In Christianity," continues De Maistre, "there is much that is high and sublime; between the priest and his people there are relations so holy and so delicate, that they can only belong to men absolutely superior to other men. Confession alone requires celibacy. Never will women—and they must be particularly considered in regard to this point—give their full confidence to a married priest. But it is not easy to write on this subject."

**Self-Condemned Churches.**—"The churches so unfortunately separated from the centre of unity were not wanting in conscience, but in strength, when they sanctioned the marriage of priests. They condemn themselves by excepting bishops, and by refusing to consecrate priests before they are married. Thus do they acknowledge the rule that no priest can marry; but they admit that, by toleration and for want of subjects, a married lay person may be ordained. By a species of sophistry which from custom no longer offends, instead of ordaining a candidate, although married, they marry him in order that he may be ordained; so that, in violating the ancient rule, they distinctly bear witness to it.

"In order to know the consequences of this fatal discipline, one must have been in a position to examine them closely. The abject state of the priesthood in the countries where it prevails cannot be understood by those who have not witnessed it. De Tott, in his Memoirs, has not said too much on this point. Who could believe that, in a country where the excellence of the marriage of priests is seriously maintained, the epithet, son of a priest, is a formal insult? Details on this matter would be highly piquant, and in some respects even useful; but it is painful to amuse malice and to afflict an unfortunate order, which contains, although everything be against it, most estimable men, as far as it is possible to form a judgment of them at the distance at which inexorable opinion holds them from all distinguished society.

TESTIMONY OF A RUSSIAN PRELATE.—"Seeking always, as far as is practicable, my arms in the camp of the enemy, I shall not pass over in silence the striking testimony of the same Russian prelate I have already quoted. We shall see what he thought of the discipline of his Church on the point of celibacy. This testimony bears with it all the weight we can possibly look for, as it not only comes to us recommended by the name of its author, but issues also from the presses of the Holy Synod

"After having repeated in the first chapter of his Prolegomena an indecent attack of Mosheim, the Archbishop de Twer continues in the following words:—

"'I believe, then, that marriage was never allowed to the doctors of the Church, (the priests) except in cases of necessity; when, for instance, the subjects who present themselves in order to fulfil those functions, not having fortitude to deny themselves marriage which they desire, better and more worthy cannot be found; so that the Church, after these incontinent persons have taken wives to themselves, admits them to holy orders by accident rather than by choice.'

"Who would not be struck by this decision of a man in such a favorable position for examining minutely what he treats of, and so hostile, besides, to the Catholic system?

THE CONSCIENCE OF MAN.—"Although it would not have cost me too much to dwell at length on the consequences of the contrary system, I cannot, however, avoid insisting on the absolute nullity of that priesthood, in its relation with the conscience of man. That wonderful influence which checked Theodosius at the entrance of the Church, Attila at the gates of Rome, and Louis XIV. before the holy table; that power, still more wonderful, which can soften the heart of the hardened sinner, and restore it to life; which enters palaces, and brings from thence the gold of the affluent—let them be never so unfeeling or distracted—to pour it into the lap of indigence; which encounters and surmounts all difficulties, whenever there is a question of consoling, of enlightening, of saving a soul;—which speaks gently but irresistibly to consciences, discovers their fatal secrets, to pluck out, together with them, the very roots of vice; the organ and guardian of holy unions; the ever-active enemy of every species of licentiousness; mild, without weakness; terrible, but loving; invaluable supplement of reason, of probity, of honor, of all the powers of man, at the moment they declare themselves powerless; precious and inexhaustible source of reconciliation, of reparations, of restitutions, of efficacious repentance, of all that God most loves after innocence itself; at his post by the cradle of man dispensing benediction; and still at his post when, standing near his deathbed, he says to him, in the midst of the most pathetic exhortations, and the most affectionate adieus, ' DEPART, CHRISTIAN SOUL.' . . . .

"'This supernatural power is nowhere to be found apart from unity. I have studied leisurely such Christianity as exists beyond this Divine pale. Its priesthood is powerless, and trembles before those whom it ought to inspire with salutary dread. To him who comes to say, ' *I have stolen,*' it dares not say, restore. The most abominable sinner owes it no promise; the priest is employed like a machine. We might suppose that his words are a kind of mechanical operation for effacing sins, as material stains are made to disappear by the application of soap; but, in order to appreciate, one must have witnessed such a state of things. The moral state of the man who has recourse to the ministry of the priest is so indifferent in those countries, and is made so little account of, that it is quite common to hear people ask one another in conversation, " *Have you been to your Easter devotions?*" This is a question like any other, to which the ready answer is *yes* or *no*, as if it were merely the case of a walk or a visit, which depends entirely on the will of him who goes to walk or to see his friends."

De Maistre points out that women, in their relations with the priesthood, cannot fail to be an object of notice to all observers. The curse is inevitable. Every married priest will always fall below his character. The incontestable superiority of the Catholic Church depends entirely on the law of celibacy.

A STARTLING ASSERTION.—The learned authors of the British Library have ventured on a startling assertion in regard to this subject, which requires to be quoted and examined.

" If the ministers of the Catholic worship," say they, " had more generally possessed the spirit of their state, in the true sense of the word, attacks against religion would not have proved so successful . . . Fortunately for the cause of religion, of morals, and the happiness of a numerous population, the English clergy, whether Anglican or Presbyterian, is far otherwise respectable, and it presents not to the enemies of public worship either the same reasons or the same pretexts."

THE WAY OF PREJUDICE.—" One might search a thousand volumes," says De Maistre, " and not meet with anything so rash; it only furnishes, however, a new proof of the terrible sway of prejudice over some of the ablest minds, and some of the most estimable men.

" In the first place, I am at a loss to know in what way the comparison is at all applicable; it can have no foundation whatever, unless priesthood be opposed to priesthood. Now there is no longer any priesthood in the Protestant churches; the priest has disappeared together with the sacrifice; and it was very remarkable that, wherever the Reformation was established, language, the unerring interpreter of the conscience, immediately abolished the word *priest*, in so much that, so early as the time of Bacon, this word was taken for a kind of insult. (Vol. iv., p. 472). When, therefore, there is mention of the clergy of England, Scotland, etc., the expression is not correct; for there is no longer *clergy*, when there are no longer clergymen; just as the military state no longer exists when there are no military. The comparison, therefore, is quite as good as if the parish priests of France and Italy had been compared to the barristers or medical practitioners of England and Scotland.

SUPERIORITY OF THE CATHOLIC CLERGY.—" But in giving to this word *clergy* all possible latitude, and holding it to be applicable to every body of ministers of Christian worship, the immense superiority of the Catholic clergy, in merit as well as in consideration, is as evident as the light of the sun.

" It may even be observed that these two kinds of superiority resolve into one; for as regards a body such as the Catholic clergy, great consideration is inseparable from great merit; and what is very remarkable, this consideration is attributed to it even in separated nations, for conscience awards it, and conscience is an incorruptible judge."

VOLTAIRE TESTIFIES.—The French statesman shows that even the censures that are addressed to the Catholic priesthood prove their superiority. Voltaire admirably says:— " The life of secular men has always been more vicious than that of priests; but the disorders of the latter have always been more remarkable, from their contrast with the rule." Nothing is forgiven them, because everything is expected of them.

"The same rule," observes De Maistre, " obtains from the Sovereign Pontiff to the sacristan. Every member of the Catholic clergy is constantly confronted with his ideal character, and constantly judged without mercy. His peccadilloes, even, are grievous misdeeds; whilst, on the other side, crimes are only slight offences, quite the same as among people of the world. What is a minister of the reformed worship? A man clothed in black, who ascends a pulpit every Sunday, to deliver a polite discourse. Every honest man may succeed in this profession, and it excludes no weakness of the honest man. I have narrowly examined this class of men; above all, I have interrogated, in regard to these evangelical ministers, the opinion immediately around them, and this opinion even I have found to agree with our own in awarding them no superiority of character.

> Ce qu'ils peuvent n'est rien; ils sont ce que nous sommes,
> Véritablement hommes,
> Et vivent comme nous.

"Nothing more than probity is required of them. But what is this merely human virtue for the formidable ministry which requires probity divinized, that is, sanctity? I might here show how I could be borne out in this statement by celebrated examples and frequent anecdotes; but this is a matter I wish to treat as if I were treading on burning coals. Let one great fact suffice, because it is public, and cannot be gainsaid: the fact of the universal decline in public opinion of the Protestant Anglical ministry. The evil is of ancient date, and is traceable to the early days of the Reformation. The celebrated Lesdiguières, who resided long on the frontiers of the duchy of Savoy, highly esteemed and saw frequently St. Francis de Sales, at that time Bishop of Geneva. The Protestant ministers, shocked at such a friendship, resolved to address an admonition in due form to the noble warrior, who was then, moreover, the chief of their party. Whoever desires to know what happened, and what was said on that occasion, may read the whole history in one of our ascetic works, which enjoys a tolerable circulation. For my part I am not copying."

DEGRADATION IN ENGLAND.—England is pointed to; but it is in England particularly that the degradation of the evangelical ministry is most obvious. The property of the clergy is almost all become the patrimony of the junior members of good families, who amuse themselves in the world, like the people of the world, leaving, moreover, to hired substitutes the task of praising God.

"The bench of bishops in the house of Peers is a kind of superfluity which might be removed without occasioning the least inconvenience. These prelates scarcely venture to speak even on matters connected with religion.

"The clergy of the second order is excluded from the national representation, and, in order to keep them always at a distance from it, recourse is had to an historical subtlety which a breath of the legislature might have removed long ago, if opinion did not, as is obvious, repel them. Not only is the clerical order lowered in public opinion, it is also mistrustful even of itself. Frequently has the English ecclesiastic been known, ashamed of his state, to efface from public writings the fatal letter (R., Rev.) which preserves his name and denotes his character. Frequently, also, has he been seen disguised as in a layman's dress, and sometimes even in military garb, figuring in drawing-rooms abroad, with his harlequin sword."

CATHOLIC EMANCIPATION.—De Maistre adds that, at the time (1805) when in England was agitated, with so much noise and solemnity, the question of Catholic emancipation, ecclesiastics were spoken of in Parliament with such bitterness, such harshness, and such decided mistrust, that strangers were, beyond comparison, more surprised than the ordinary audience.

It must be said also that there is, even in the character of this evangelical militia, something that forbids confidence, and invokes discredit. There is no authority, no rule, and consequently no common belief in their churches. They themselves acknowledge with perfect candor, "that the Protestant ecclesiastic is not obliged to subscribe any confession of faith whatever, except for the sake of public repose and tranquillity, without any other object than to maintain between the members of the same community EXTERNAL union; but that in other respects none of these confessions can be considered, properly speaking, a rule of faith. Protestants recognize no other than the Holy Scripture.

"When, therefore, one of these preachers goes to preach, what means has he of proving that he believes what he says? and what means has he, moreover, of knowing that his audience is making light of him? I cannot avoid thinking I hear every one of his hearers saying to him with a sceptic grin, truly I believe that he believes that I believe him.

WARBURTON'S BLIND HATRED.—" One of the most hardened fanatics that ever existed, Warburton, founded," says the distinguished French author, "at his death, a chair to prove that the Pope is Antichrist. To the shame of our unfortunate nature, this chair has not yet been vacant. There was seen advertised in the English newspapers of this year (1817) a discourse delivered on account of the foundation. I do not at all believe in the good faith of Warburton; but, although it were possible on the part of one man, how imagine a succession of extravagant persons, all gone wrong in the same way—all raving in sincerity! Common sense totally rejects such a conclusion; so that, without the least doubt, several, perhaps all, will have spoken for money against their conscience. Only fancy a Pitt, a Fox, a Burke, a Grey, a Granville, or other minds of the like calibre, attending one of these sermons! Not only must the preacher be lost in their estimation, discredit will also reflect on the whole order of preachers.

I speak here of a particular case; but there are many other causes which wound the character of the dissenting ecclesiastic, and lower him in opinion. It is impossible that men, habitually mistrusted, can enjoy much consideration; never will they be looked upon, by their own party even, otherwise than as advocates paid to support a certain cause. They will never be denied talent, science, punctuality in the fulfilment of their duties; sincerity is quite another thing.

GIBBON ON THE REFORMED CHURCH.—"The doctrine of a reformed Church," says Gibbon, "has nothing in common with the knowledge or the belief of those who are connected with it, and the modern clergy subscribe, with a sigh or smile, the forms of orthodoxy and established symbols.... The predictions of the Catholics have come to be fulfilled. The Armenians, the Arians, the Socinians, whose members cannot be calculated according to their respective congregations, have broken and rejected the connected series of the mysteries of revelation."

" Gibbon here," remarks De Maistre, " expresses the universal opinion of enlightened Protestants in regard to their clergy. I have had many opportunities of knowing this fact, and have learned it for certain. There is, therefore, no medium for the reformed minister. If he preaches dogma, men believe that he is retailing falsehood; if he dare not preach it, they do not believe that he is anything.

MERELY CIVIL OFFICERS.—"The sacred character having been wholly obliterated from the brow of those ministers, sovereigns no longer considered them otherwise than as civil officers, whose duty it was to follow, together with the rest of the flock, under the common crook. The touching complaints uttered even by a member of this unfortunate order on the way in which temporal authority makes use of their ministry, will not be read without interest. After having declaimed, like a vulgar man, against the Catholic hierarchy, he soars of a sudden above all prejudices, and pronounces these solemn words:—

"'Protestantism has not less vilified the sacerdotal dignity. In order not to seem to aspire to the Catholic hierarchy, the Protestant priests divested themselves very speedily of all religious appearance, and placed themselves most humbly at the feet of the temporal authority. . . . Because it was by no means the vocation of the Protestant priests to govern the state, it ought not thence to have been concluded that it belonged to the state to rule the Church. . . . The salaries which the state awards to ecclesiastics have rendered them quite worldly . . . together with their sacerdotal robes, they have cast off the spiritual character. . . The state has done its work, and all the evil must be laid to the charge of the Protestant clergy. It has become frivolous. . . . The priests do no more than to fulfil their duties as citizens. . . . The state no longer views them in any other light than as officers of police. . . . It has little esteem for them and assigns to them the lowest rank among its officers. . . . when religion becomes the servant of the state, it is permitted to look upon it in this degraded condition as the work of men, and even as a deception. In our days only have industry, diet, politics, rural economy, and police been known to enter the pulpit. . . . The priest must believe that he follows out his destiny and fulfils his duties in giving a lecture from the pulpit on the regulations of the police. He must publish in his sermons receipts against epizootic, show the necessity of vaccination, and preach on the means of prolonging human life. How, then, after this, will he set about diverting men's affections from temporal and perishable things, whilst he himself endeavors, with the sanction of government, to attach them to the galleys of life.'"

## CHAPTER V.

### Curbing the Passions.

Voluntary Austerities Among the Manicheans, Buddhists, and Brahmans—Lessons to Protestants—Monasteries and Nunneries—Their Early Establishment and Magnificent Work.

One of the doctrines of Luther is that it is impossible for man to curb certain passions. He alludes to concupiscence. His imitators have echoed and reechoed this "sentiment" and have used it—often in shameful ways—as an argument against priestly celibacy. How many precious souls have been lost through making this horrible doctrine an excuse for doing what their inner consciousness tells them is wrong. The history of the world proves the contrary. We will give examples, not only from the lives of the early Christians, but from the history of pagans, to prove that man can and has curbed his passions. Men, even without the blessed light of the true gospel, have voluntarily retired from the world to practise virtues that put the Protestant Christianity of our own times to the blush.

Universal Respect for Virtue.—Everywhere and in all times, virtue has claimed the respect of even the worst elements of mankind. The rulers of the Church saw how it would add to the usefulness of the clergy, how it would enhance their value in the eyes of the people, if, by their fortitude and self-abnegation, they became continent, mortified the flesh and gave an example of the attainment of salvation by the sacrifice of passions and affections. When Christianity dawned upon the world, society was wholly corrupt. Licentiousness was the order of the day. The satirists and historians of the Roman empire give proof of it. Unchastity was thought to be no crime, purity was the laughing stock of the so-called wits. A new system of morality was imperative to save society. The early Christians were at first a puzzle to the vicious, and in time they became objects of admiration, then of hatred, and again of admiration. Justin Martyr, the Apologist, who flourished about 150, refers to their chastity and sobriety thus:—

"Quid enim, enumeremus infinitam multitudinem eorum qui ab incontinenti intemperataque vita abducti sunt quum hæc ipsa didicissent?"

[How can we enumerate the infinite multitude of those who, when they learned these things, gave up a life of unchastity and intemperance?]

THE RISE OF ASCETICISM.—When converts had their eyes opened to the sinfulness of their lives, naturally they were tempted to plunge into the other extreme. Hence the rise of asceticism. The practical morality of the Gospel was perverted by converted philosophers, and heresies resulted. The Abstinentes, the Apotactici, the Excalceati, and other sects denounced marriage as a deadly sin. For fully 300 years before the birth of Christ Buddhism was the chief religion of India. It was a religion of asceticism. It is curious how many of its observances and customs are analogous to those of Christianity.' It is said that monasticism, the tonsure, the use of rosaries, confession, penance, absolution, and other practices are derived from Buddhism.

MONASTIC INSTITUTIONS DEVELOPED.—The general advance of the Church at this period (312-476) was followed by the development of monastic institutions. Monks were at first divided into three classes: the Cenobites, who lived in communities under a superior; the Anchorites, who lived alone in the desert solitudes; the Sabaraites, who lived two or three together in cells; the latter class had but little duration. Cassian has drawn a graphic picture of the edifying life led by the solitaries of his day. They were wholly occupied in prayer and manual labor; their daily food was bread and water; their bed, a rush mat; their pillow, a handful of leaves.

Egypt was the birth place of the monastic life; from thence it passed into Syria, Pontus, Asia Minor, and the West. Then the Gauls had also their celebrated monasteries, among which may be mentioned the foundation of those of Tours and of Lerins. The name of St. Augustine is also associated with a code of monastic rules destined to lead generations of religious to the height of sanctity.

Most of the monks were laymen, and Cassian tells us that those of St. Pacomius's monastery depended upon the priests of the neighboring villages for the celebration of the Holy Mysteries. The monastic life debarred them from the priestly state. The manual labor to which they devoted themselves furnished them not only the means of procuring their coarse and slender fare, but even of giving plentiful alms. The Alexandrian poor were relieved by boat loads of wheat which had been raised from the burning sands of the desert by the patient toil of the monks of Arsinoë. St. Augustine notices the same practical charity in the monks of Northern Africa. Yet some of these solitaries were occasionally torn from their desert homes to be incorporated among the clergy of the neighboring episcopal city; but they then became seculars, as was the case with those who were raised to the episcopate. In his letter to Dracontius, written about the year 353, St. Athanasius reckons seven monks who had already been made bishops. Such was the increase of solitaries at the end of the fourth century, that the single City of Oxyrinchus, in Lower Thebais, numbered ten thousand monks and twenty thousand virgins.

COMMUNITIES OF WOMEN.—It would seem that the formation of communities of women preceded those of men. St. Anthony, when about to begin his solitary life, first placed his sister in a convent of virgins (παρθενῶνα). Tertullian and Cyprian both speak of this community of women as having been long established.

The monastic institutions were divided into five classes—Monks, Canons Regular, Military Orders, Friars, and Clerks Regular.

THE FOUNDER OF CŒNOBITIC LIFE.—When St. Anthony died in 365, aged 105, the desert was already studded with hermitages in every direction, and the second great step in the development of monasticism had been long taken by Pachomius, who is regarded as the founder of the cœnobitic life amongst Christians, and as the author of the first formal monastic rule. Pachomius was born about 292. While serving in the army he was converted to Christianity, and on his discharge adopted the ascetic life under the hermit Palæmon, with whom he retired to Tabernæ, an island in the Nile, between Farshoot and Denderah. There he elaborated his system. A strict probation of three years was imposed upon postulants for admission.

He induced his sister to found a convent of nuns governed by rules like his own, and subject to the authority of a visitor appointed by himself, as superior of the noble institute. When he died (between 348 and 360) he had no fewer than 1,400 monks in his own monastery, and 7,000 altogether under his authority. St. Athanasius introduced his system into Italy, and finally it was displaced by the Benedictine Order.

THE DIGNITY OF LABOR.—One of the most valuable features in the rule of St. Benedict was the restoration of the dignity of labor. In his days toil of all kinds was considered degrading, and was done by slaves. By making it a part of his monastic system, he elevated labor and dignified the toiler. A Protestant writer, the Rev. R. F. Littledale, said of him:—" It is the special glory of Benedict that he taught the men of his day that work, sanctified by prayer, is the best thing which man can do, and the lesson has never been wholly lost sight of since."

The same writer says of this famous Order:—" It was as teachers of what for those times was scientific agriculture, as drainers of fens and morasses, as clearers of forests, as makers of roads, as tillers of the reclaimed soil, as architects of durable and even stately buildings, as exhibiting a visible type of orderly government, as establishing the superiority of peace over war as the normal condition of life, as students in the library which the rule sets up in every monastery, as the masters in schools, open not merely to their own postulants, but to the children of secular families also, that they won their high place in history, as benefactors of mankind."

WOMEN ELEVATED.—Of the nuns Mr. Littledale says:—" The cloister was not alone the single secure shelter for women who had no strong arm to rely on, but it provided the only alternative profession to marriage, and that one recognized by public opinion as of even higher destination, and opening to women positions of substantial rank and authority, less precarious than the possession of temporal estates, which might only serve to attract cupidity, and so invite attack. The abbess of a great Benedictine house was more than the equal of the wife of any save a very great noble; and as single women were thus not obliged to look to wedlock as the only path to safety and consequence, they were enabled to mate on more equal terms, and were less likely to be viewed as the mere toys or servants of the stronger sex."

TESTIMONY OF A PROTESTANT.—But nowhere do we find in this Protestant author who has written on "Monachism" such terrible and vile slanders of his kind, as have been recently uttered by another Protestant clergyman. He does not speak degradingly of these noble women and these holy men, for the reason that he had studied his subject, and had brought a cultivated mind to bear upon it. On the contrary, he says, touching upon the Reformation period in England:—

"There is little reason to trust the charge of immorality brought against the monks, when Henry VIII. had once resolved on the pillage of the monasteries. The characters of the king himself, of Cromwell, his chief agent in the dissolution, and of Layton, Legh, and others of the visitors appointed to inquire into the condition of the houses, are such as to deprive their statements of all credit; and, besides, the earlier Act of dissolution, granted the smaller monasteries to the king, limits the charges of misconduct to them, expressly acquitting the larger houses. Nevertheless, when the appetite for plunder had increased with the first taste of booty, accusations of precisely the same sort were brought up against the great monasteries, though in no instance has any verifiable proof been preserved."

SUPPRESSIONS IN ENGLAND.—The number of houses suppressed and overthrown in England by the two Acts of 1536 and 1538 was as follows:—186 Benedictine houses, 173 Augustinians, 101 Cistercians, 33 Dominican, Franciscan, Carmelite, and Austin friaries, 32 Præmonstratensians, 28 Knights Hospitalers, 25 Gilbertines, 20 Cluniacs, 9 Carthusians, 3 Frontevraud, 3 Minoresses, 2 Bonhommes, 1 Brigittine; total, 616.

THE MANICHÆANS.—There were two great religious systems opposed to Catholicism in Western Asia and the South of Europe, at the close of the third century. These were Manichæism and Neo-Platonism, and, like the Catholic religion, they had put off the national and particular character of the ancient religions, and tried to become universal. What is true of Manichæism is to a great extent true of Neo-Platonism.

Manichæism had ideas of revelation, redemption, ascetic virtue, and morality. Manichæism survived until far into the middle ages. The founder of the system was Mani, a highborn Persian of Ecbatana. The ethics of Manichæism were thoroughly ascetic. The eating of the flesh of animals and the drinking of wine were forbidden. Especially was every gratification of sexual desire, and hence also marriage, forbidden. Life was further regulated by an exceedingly rigorous system of fasts. Certain astronomical conjunctions determined the selection of the fast days, which in their total number amounted to nearly a quarter of the year. Sunday was always one. Hours of prayer were determined with equal exactness. The Manichæans had to pray four times a day, each prayer being preceded by ablutions.

FALSE ASSERTIONS.—And yet Protestants say it is impossible for man to curb his passions. But here, hundreds and hundreds of years ago, were multitudes of men without the light of the true Gospel, without the graces which Christianity bestows, living lives that apparently were examples of purity, and with naught to sustain them but the consciousness of right.

It is held that the later Manichæans celebrated mysteries analogous to Christian baptism and the Lord's Supper. What knowledge Mani had of Christianity, or how it reached him, cannot be easily determined. The Western Manichæans of the fourth and fifth centuries are much more like Christians than their Eastern brethren. What gave strength to Manichæism was rather that it undid an ancient mythology and a thorough-going materialistic dualism with an exceedingly spiritual worship as well as strict morality.

THE BUDDHISTS.—Let us turn to India for another example of how men can curb their passions. Buddhism formerly prevailed through a large part of that great country. It is now professed by the inhabitants of Ceylon, Siam, and Burmah (the Southern Buddhists), and of Nepaul, Thibet, China, and Japan, (the Northern Buddhists.) It arose out of the philosophical and ethical teachings of Siddhârta Gautama, the eldest son of Suddhôdana, who was Rajah in Kapilavastu and chief of the tribe of the Sâkyas, an Aryan clan seated during the fifth century, B. C., on the banks of the Kohona, about 100 miles north of the city of Benares, and about fifty miles north of the foot of the Himalaya Mountains.

It was a logical conclusion from the views of life

held by Gautama that any rapid progress in spiritual life was only compatible with an ascetic life, in which all such contact with the world as would tend to create earthly desires would be reduced as much as possible.

CONTRARY TO LUTHER.—This is contrary to the teachings of Luther, which we abundantly show elsewhere.

Buddhism taught that to forsake the world was a necessary step towards the attainment of spiritual freedom. Those who devoted themselves to the higher life gradually assumed the characteristics of the monks of Christianity. Rules were laid down and followed. No monk could eat solid food, except between sunrise and noon, and total abstinence from intoxicating drinks was rendered obligatory. The majority of the monks lived in companies in groves or gardens, and very soon the piety of laymen provided for them suitable monasteries, several of which were built even in the lifetime of Buddha. Poor and scanty clothing was provided for them.

Sexual intercourse was looked upon as the blackest of sins, and the offender was expelled from the order. The vow of poverty was taken and the monk was allowed only eight simple articles. Self-conquest and universal charity were the foundations of the system. In the eighth and ninth centuries a great persecution arose, and the Buddhists were so utterly exterminated that there is not now a Buddhist in all India, although, of course, the effects of so great a movement could not pass away, and it left its mark for ever on the Hinduism which supplanted it.

THE BRAHMANS.—The new theistic church in India, Brahmanism, owes its origin to Rajah Ram Mohan Rai, one of the leading men whom India has produced in later times. Impressed with the fallacy of the religious ceremonies practised by his countrymen, he impartially investigated the Hindu Shastras, the Koran, and the Bible, and inculcated the reformed principles of monotheism. In 1830, he organized a Hindu society for prayer-meetings, which may be considered as the foundation of the present Brahma Samaj. Austere practices were enjoined to fit one's self for a departure from this life. Orthodox Brahmanical scholasticism made the attainment of final emancipation dependent on perfect knowledge of the divine essence. This knowledge could be obtained only by complete abstraction of the mind from external objects and intense meditation on the divinity, brought about by the total extinction of all sensual instincts by means of austerity. The Brahman occupied a high rank among the Hindus because the people believed him to be a pure, stainless being.

# CHAPTER VI.

## The Confessional.

BITTER ATTACKS UPON IT BY PROTESTANTS—IGNORANT AND FANATICAL CONTROVERSIALISTS—A DIVINE INSTITUTION—RULES OF THE CHURCH IN CONFESSING WOMEN AND CHILDREN—THE MORAL THEOLOGY SIDE OF THE QUESTION.

By far the bitterest attacks of the Protestants have been directed against the Confessional. They merely scoff at the other sacraments of the Church, but of the Sacrament of Penance their condemnation is strong, their hate deep, bitter, and lasting. Of all the harsh and vile things they have said of the monasteries and nunneries, they cannot compare, singly or wholly, with the nastiness and gratuitous falsehoods with which they have assailed the confessional.

A POWER IN THE CHURCH.—Instinctively they feel this is one of the greatest powers the Church wields to preserve its members from the contamination of the world, the continuance of the indulgence of passion, the taint of heresy.

If confession were a human institution, perhaps the attacks upon it would not be so venomous. It is essentially **supernatural**, and therefore mere human arguments against it are instinctively felt to be unavailing. They cannot point to any one man as its founder, to any particular period in history when its appearance, surprised a community. It always existed. It is of divine origin. Christ was its founder. "Confess your sins to one another," was said at the beginning.

HUMAN PRIDE REBELS.—It is a hard thing for man to say, "I have done wrong—I have sinned." Human pride rebels against the confession. Rare is the estimable man—estimable in all things but pride—who will blushingly declare—in public or to his neighbor—"I have done wrong in this thing." He will give money, to repair an injustice, but he will not say in so many words —"I have done an injustice."

Examples are thick around us of this stubborness of heart. The readers of newspapers, day after day, see accounts of strikes all over the country, all over the world. Workmen have been underpaid. They have been unjustly deprived of a fair share of the fruits of their labor. When the public cry goes up, does the master or the corporation say, " we have been unjust, come back, we will do better in the future."

No. They may have the feeling, but their pride revolts against the confession; they will not acknowledge a fault, and they would rather continue the bitter fight against justice to the poor and lowly, rather lose all they had gained, than stand before the world self-accused. It is the weakness of human nature.

SPIRITUAL PRIDE.—This being true in worldly matters, how much more so is it in spiritual. It is the same kind of stubborness that prevents the man kneeling in the confessional and confessing his sins against his Maker. He is too proud to say, "I have committed this fault—forgive me." Deep down in his heart he has the consciousness of sin, but he is afraid to put it into words.

There may be, too, a sense of shame. But if this

shame can be overcome, if the penitent can be brought to confess, how great is the victory! He feels like a new man; he is comforted; he is strengthened. He is strong in a resolve to sin no more. The very pain of making the confession will linger with him, and when next the occasion of sin arises, the memory of the smart will be present, and he will resist the temptation. The child that has been scorched by fire will avoid the flame.

CONFESSION NEVER EASY.—He must know little or nothing of human nature, or be wilfully blind, or close his eyes to what he sees, who dares to assert that the frequency of confession dulls the sense of shame in the penitent, and renders him more indifferent to the hideousness of sin. In common parlance, one never becomes used to it. The confession is always an ordeal —even to the best of men and women. There is the examination of conscience, trying in itself, while the laying bare of the heart to another—even though penitent and confessor may not see each other, is no grateful task. True, the penitent knows that he is confessing to Almighty God, and that the priest is but the agent of the Sacrament of Penance. Yet it is the humiliating confession of weakness. This is partly a human way of looking at it, but the argument is that the act of going to confession and the necessity of exciting within one's self a lively contrition, before absolution can be received, is just as much a deterrent from sin as are the legal punishments in the case of crime in the world, nay, more so.

PROTESTANT CONFESSION.—How comfortable and easy is the confession of the Protestant. All that is required of him is to feel within his own heart that he is a sinner, and he is "saved." He has no apt and instant words of comfort, advice, and guidance from a priest who has studied the soul, who has devoted himself to its service, and who is gifted with the grace to lead it into the straight and narrow path.

And men are found in this enlightened age to aver that the confessional is the corrupter of youth and women. To say so is one thing; to prove it, is another.

DOCTRINE OF CONFESSION.— The doctrine of the Church is no secret. She teaches and has always taught that, for the pardon of sins in the Sacrament of Penance, Christ requires the penitent's confession, with contrition and satisfaction, and the priest's absolution. No confession, however full, will obtain pardon for sin, unless the person confessing is sorry for having committed it and resolves to amend. The Church teaches that the Sacrament of Penance is necessary for all those who have committed any mortal sin after baptism.

The person who worthily frequents confession gains a firm purpose of amendment, the marks of which are a change of life, the avoiding of the occasions that commonly lead to sin, and the endeavor to destroy evil habits.

CONTRITION NECESSARY.—The Church teaches that contrition should have four qualities—interior, supernatural, universal, and sovereign. By interior sorrow is meant that it is in the heart and is sincere—otherwise it would be only hypocrisy. Supernatural sorrow should be produced in the heart by a motive of faith and the grace of the Holy Ghost. Universal sorrow should extend to all our mortal sins. By sovereign is meant that we be more grieved for having offended God than for all the other evils that could happen to us. Perfect contrition is a hearty sorrow for having offended God, because he is sovereignly good, and it has the effect of justifying the sinner by itself, and before absolution, yet with the desire and obligation of confessing as soon as possible.

Imperfect contrition, commonly called attrition, is a hearty sorrow for having offended God on account of the shamefulness of having sin, or the fear of its punishment, which is the eternal pains of hell. Though attrition disposes the penitent for obtaining pardon of his sins, yet it is better to excite himself as far as he is able to perfect contrition, before confession.

AN INSULT TO THE MORAL SENSE.—All that a priest teaches almost every day. But ah! says the fanatic, the confessional is the corrupter of youth and women. Indeed! Is it not an insult to human intelligence to believe that 200,000,000 people, of all races and all languages, can be cajoled by a corrupt institution? Is it not an insult to the moral sense of intelligent beings to assert that they willingly, gladly, give themselves up to a vile machine, to be made infamous and diabolical? The supposition is monstrous.

The unfortunate men who speak thus have not unfrequently paid tribute to the eloquence of the Catholic priest and have never denied that the pulpit discourses have been at least moral and full of exhortations to virtue, and denunciations of vice. "Ah! but they were hypocrites—they did not practise what they preached." Well, it will be acknowledged that we are not all born devils. Most of the congregations to whom the priest preaches are young, and are yet innocent of the worst of sins, especially the young woman. How great then would be the shock these would experience at discovering in the confessional the very opposite of what they had heard in the pulpit!

BOURDALOUE'S INSTRUCTION.—Listen to the eloquence of a Bourdaloue on this very subject of the sacrament of penance:—

"But how shall we begin to discern in ourselves this true penitence, and what I here call a sincere and efficacious detestation of sin? Hearken Christians, and judge by this practical induction. By actually and effectually cutting off whatever we discover in ourselves to be the cause of sin, or fomenting and nourishing that body of sin which God, at our conversion, wills us to destroy. By relinquishing a thousand agreeable things, the carnal man's delight, but which, for that reason, are incentives to evil and poison to the soul. By declining those objects that excite in the heart pernicious desires, which, according to the Scripture, 'when concupiscence conceiveth, it bringeth forth sin.' By a scrupulous carefulness of avoiding conversations, of which we know how the baneful licentiousness corrupts and enfeebles purity of manners, as they give occasion to the first wounds, and not unfrequently the most incurable, that sin inflicts. By a severe, salutary, necessary resolution of giving up such intercourses as we know by experience are the bonds of sin; exhibitions and spectacles the effect of which is to stir up in the heart the most lively passions, and to diffuse in the imagination the most dangerous ideas, the seeds of immorality; assemblies and routs, in which the spirit of impurity reigns, and can lay inevitable snares for innocence; romances and novels, by which our curiosity is so justly punished by the malignant impression they leave behind. * * * In a word, by that evangelical circumcision which stops not at outward show and alterations, but searches the inmost recesses of the heart, and destroys radically every efficient of sin it meets with.

THE METHOD OF HYPOCRISY.—"The method of hypocrisy," Bourdaloue said in the same sermon, "is to lament the violent attacks of passion, and yet rush into the dangers blindly, and inconsiderately, in which passions the most moderate are hardly governable. The method of hypocrisy is to cry, 'oh! unhappy man that I am! born so sensual and so frail!' and to seek, notwithstanding this open acknowledgment, occasions of sinning against God's command, in which human frailty, from a mere misfortune, becomes a crime, or at least the original of all crimes. Such is the nature of penitential hypocrisy; and that is the judgment you ought to form of it. * * * The efficacy, therefore, of penance, consists in generously quitting the occasion of sin, in order to overcome it; and not attempting to overcome it by sluggishly remaining in the occasion of it."

NO CHANCE FOR THE WOULD-BE-CORRUPTER.—Do these utterances sound like the words of a hypocrite? Can this priest be the corrupter of youth and of women in the confessional? But if the Protestant will concede that Bourdaloue was above reproach, what chance would a priest of wicked heart have of corrupting those who listened to such exhortations as Bourdaloue's, and who had been instructed in their faith? None whatever. His penitents would fly from him in horror. He would be discovered, denounced, and driven from the priesthood.

It is charged that those studying for the priesthood in seminaries are corrupted by being forced to study certain theological works dealing with confession. It is one of those calumnies that we are always meeting; it is a kind of mud the enemies of the Church are always hurling at it, in the vain hope that some of it will stick. As a matter of fact, the young men in the seminaries are not only not induced to study these subjects, but they are deterred from studying them until they shall have received sacred orders. Then their age is more advanced, and they are not likely to be affected injuriously by that special study. So careful are the instructors in this respect that the treatises on marriage and the sixth commandment, known as the Diaconale—that is, that portion of theology studied only after the student has entered into deacon's orders—are kept away from the novice, like the custom among the Jews, who forbade the reading of the "Canticle of Canticles" until a certain age had been attained.

KEPT AWAY FROM THE STUDENT.—The great aim is to keep young men away from that kind of theology. It is not taught in classes. In the seminaries in Rome it is not taught at all. But when they go out to assume the duties of the priest they have these works to consult when occasion requires.

The priest beginning his mission must know something about souls, their trials, and their needs. There is no such thing (and it is a pity there is not) as ready made experience in any calling. The young priest must be qualified to guide his penitents. Otherwise it is the blind leading the blind. His knowledge he must gain from books.

CASE OF THE PHYSICIAN AND SURGEON.—Is it not the same with the physician and surgeon? Would any sane person advocate the burning of every book of medicine or surgery that treated of certain diseases and delicate matters, on the ground that they tended to corrupt the student? Is it not just as illogical to say, destroy these special theological works, they are dangerous, as to say, destroy the medical books, they are vicious?

The new priest is specially instructed that the moral theology questions are not to be asked on those delicate subjects. Theologians lay down the rule that it is better that the penitent even omit some sins rather than that there shall be any risk run of corrupting the young mind by suggesting certain sins.

GUARDING CHILDREN.—In the case of the child the rule is laid down that the confessor should be so careful that he should not leave the least bad impression after confession, and that the confession should be imperfect rather than that the confessor should touch upon what was not known before.

There is nothing in the whole practice of the Church in which she is more careful than in this matter of the confessional.

But supposing a priest should be so utterly depraved as to wish to corrupt souls, at the very beginning he would run the danger of involving himself in much difficulty. The discipline of the Church has provided for such a contingency. In the punishment awarded both parties are included. The moment a confessor suggests a sin to a penitent, that instant his jurisdiction over it ceases. He has no power to absolve from that particular sin, and the penitent must seek another confessor. These are facts that Protestants should know.

CANONICAL CENSURES.—In 1869 Pope Pius IX. ordered the theologians to go over the censures of the Church and make out a list of them. In Chapter 4 it is decreed that excommunication is incurred, *ipso facto*, by the person concurring in the sin, "by those who neglect, or who culpably omit to denounce, within a month, the confessor or priest by whom they have been solicited to acts of wickedness." These cases are expressed in the Constitution of Gregory XV., August,

1622, and in that of Benedict XIV., June 1, 1741. Benedict XIV., says:—

"Priests, whether secular or regular, however exempt from the authority of the bishops, of whatsoever dignity or prominence they may be, who will urge any penitent —no matter who the person, man or women—either in the act of sacramental confession, or before it, or immediately after it, on the occasion of confession, or pretext of confession, or outside of the occasion of confession, in the confessional, or in any place appointed for the hearing of confession under the pretence of hearing confession there, to acts of wickedness, or who will attempt to solicit to acts of wickedness, or to solicit or to urge by words, signs, or nods, by touch, by writing to be read then or afterward, or who will have had with such persons improper and wicked conversations, are immediately deprived of jurisdiction over that person to absolve, and the person so solicited is obliged, within one month from the time of knowing the obligation, to denounce such confessor to the bishop."

THE PENITENT'S PLAIN DUTY.—Can anything be stronger or plainer than this? The person solicited is obliged to go before the bishop, and if the person does not, then he or she incurs excommunication. The bishop explains the canon law to the penitent and states that, if the person is telling an untruth, the sin is so great that no one except the Pope can give absolution. The person's statement is taken down under oath and the name of the confessor is exacted. The priest is then warned and on a third offence incurs perpetual punishment, which the Church has the power to inflict, and can never again say Mass.

The rule in Canon Law is that nothing can be established except by two or three witnesses, following the direction of St. Paul. It is easily understood how women may be jealous and induced to make false accusations. It is only one person's word against another, but two or three establish the case.

SEAL OF CONFESSION.—On the other hand, the seal of confession is always maintained. If a third party makes an accusation against a priest the confessor is never asked the name of a penitent and there is not a single instance of violation of the seal on record. But if the penitent will not give the name of the priest that person cannot obtain absolution.

Can the Church do more than this to keep the wolves from the fold?

St. Alphonsus Liguori, although by some regarded as a lax theologian, is most severe on impurity. Every act of his life, every word he has written, proves how dear to him was chastity. But some fanatical, misguided Protestants call him the corrupter of youth. When his followers, the Redemptorist Fathers, first entered Austria, they found that fornication and adultery were so common as not to cause comment. These sins they set themselves to denounce at once, and so vigorously did they do so, that they incurred the severest persecution, and it was sought to drive them from the Empire. If St. Liguori had taught otherwise the Redemptorists would not have subjected themselves, in the cause of virtue, to so much suffering. It is a good thing to know a little history when entering into a controversy.

IN THE FRENCH REVOLUTION.—When the teachings of Voltaire, Rousseau, and the so-called philosophers of the seventeenth and eighteenth centuries culminated in the French Revolution, when the streets ran with the blood of the innocent, who were the most numerous victims? The priests and the nuns. If those women were as depraved as fanatical Protestants aver, would they have so readily given up their life when they could have easily escaped by ministering to the passions of their tyrants. The religious women of France emulated the intrepidity of the priests in the prisons and on the scaffold; and those whom the revolutionary tempest had dispersed among foreign nations, and even in America, far from yielding to the most dangerous seducements, were everywhere admired for their attachment to their state of life, their respect for their vows, and the voluntary exercise of every virtue.

A Protestant who makes a sincere inquiry into the practice of confession will find that his objections are ill grounded. How many have recourse to a lawyer to be guided in the most delicate affairs of life. To him clients will lay bare all their secrets, fearing to withhold anything lest, in doing so, their lawyer would not be able to give the best counsel, and the interests of the client suffer. Any veteran counsellor will tell you that women are fonder of going to law than the men are. It is also a fact that they do not so readily disclose everything as the stronger sex do, but then the task of the lawyer is easier in finding out from women all that he wants or needs to know.

COMPARED WITH LAWYERS—Now the newspapers have published many and many a sad tale of the abuse of their position by lawyers. Numerous scandals have arisen from the intercourse of lawyer and female client. Married men as well as single men have taken advantage of their position and the confidence reposed in them to seduce, elope with, commit bigamy with their fair clients, or defraud them of their property. And yet, how unreasonable it would be for any man or set of men to blame the legal profession in general for the guilt of some of its members? How absurd it would be to petition a legislature to abolish the legal profession?

THE DISINTERESTED PRIEST AND JUDGE.—The priest is the counsellor of the soul. It is still more unreasonable, more absurd, to clamor for the abolition of his office. The troubled heart, the sinful soul, the doubting mind must turn to some one for comfort and for guidance. Who better fitted to afford it than the priest, who is specially trained, mentally and spiritually, for such a purpose? The Church protects the sinner against self-delusion—for he who is his own lawyer has a fool for his client. There are ill-gotten goods to be restored, reconciliation is to be made with enemies, forgiveness of injuries to be insisted on, calumny to be retracted, and the occasions of sin to be avoided, and all these things the confessor knows how to adjust, and is not prejudiced by self-interest or the hope of pecuniary reward, as the lawyer or a lay person would be.

A LABORIOUS DUTY.—At the same time, as has been well observed by writers on this subject, the priest affords the best protection against despair or indiscreet zeal. There is little in the laborious work of the confessional to satisfy curiosity, for the priest learns nothing except the number and species of sins committed, and he is bound, under the most sacred obligations, to abstain from all unnecessary questions, particularly from all such as might convey knowledge of sins previously unknown to the penitent. "He has," says an authority, "to decide according to the principles of an elaborate casuistry, which he has studied for years, and in which he has been examined by his superiors, before he enters the confessional. There is little room for tyranny on his part, for the faithful know well that they may have recourse to any approved pastor."

This is the very hardest work a priest has to perform —harder even than going out in a storm, or in the bitter cold on a winter's night, to a sick call. It is a fearful monotonous duty, and involves great self-denying devotion. Seldom has the confessional been polluted by human weakness and sin.

# CHAPTER VII.

## Schismatical Churches.

The Greek, Russian, Armenian, Coptic, and others—All have Married Priests, and consequently a Low Condition of Morals—Mere Puppets of the Government.

It may be well here to glance at the churches which have separated from Rome. The great Greek schism has been the parent of others. It will be noted that every schismatical Church has married priests, and that the communities in which the schismatical married priests flourish have a low degree of civilization, and that the ruling powers in the different countries make a mere puppet show of the state religion.

The Greeks and Celibacy—But first we may rapidly sketch the changes which the law of celibacy has undergone among the Greeks. In the time of the Church historian Socrates, (about 450) the same law of clerical celibacy which obtained among the Latins was observed in Thessaly, Macedonia, and Achæa. Further, the case of Synesius, in 410, proves that it was unusual for bishops to live as married men, for he had, on accepting his election as bishop, to make a stipulation that he should be allowed to live with his wife. The Synod of Trullo (692) required bishops, if married, to separate from their wives, and forbade clerics to marry after sub-deaconate.

A SLIGHT CONCESSION.—However, a law of Leo the Wise, (861–911) permitted such sub-deacons, deacons, and priests who had married after receiving their respective orders, not, indeed, to exercise sacred functions, but still to remain in the ranks of the clergy and exercise such offices, *e. g.*, matters of administration, as were consistent with the marriage which they had concluded.

The practical consequences of these enactments are (1) that Greek candidates for the priesthood usually leave the seminaries before being ordained deacons, and return having concluded marriage, commonly with daughters of clergymen; (2) that secular priests live as married men, but cannot, on the death of their wife marry again; (3) that bishops are usually chosen from the monks.

## RUSSIAN AND RUTHENIAN CHURCHES.

The Russian Church is a sad example of the degradation into which a clergy may fall through a contempt for celibacy. We have devoted the chapter following this to a description of the schismatical Russian Church.

The Ruthenians are descendants of converts from the Russian Church who have kept their old rites and dicipline. The name " Ruthenian Catholics " is given to Christians who use the Greek liturgy translated into the Old Slavonic, but who render obedience to the Pope.

The Metropolitan See of Kiev and its suffragan dioceses were united to the Catholic Church, but the union was never satisfactory and the last trace of it had disappeared early in the 16th century. The cause of union, however, was zealously promoted by the Jesuit school established at Vilna by Father Possevin, and by the Polish King Calixtus III. In 1595, the

Metropolitan of Kiev and seven suffragans were, at their own request, received by Clement VIII. into the Catholic communion.

UNDER RUSSIAN DOMINION.—Thus the Ruthenian Province arose; the Metropolitan was chosen by the bishops, and all were placed under Propaganda, which was represented by the Polish nuncio. But at the partition of Poland all the Catholic Ruthenian dioceses, except Lemberg, Przemysl, and part of Brezk, became Russian dominion. In 1795, Russia suppressed all the dioceses but one; in 1798, three dioceses were tolerated, a fourth in 1809, two only by Nicholas, in 1828. In 1839, three bishops joined the schismatic Russians, and there was, till lately, only one see of the United Ruthenians in Russian Poland, viz., Chelm and Belz—immediately subject to the Pope. At present there is another bishopric—viz., Minsk—suffragan to Mohilew. There were, in 1865, about 250,000 Catholics of the Ruthenian rite in Russian Poland. The See of Suprasl was erected in 1799, for the Ruthenians in Prussian Poland; they numbered about 40,000.

IN AUSTRIA.—In the Austrian Territory the See of Lemberg, with its suffragan sees of Przemysl, Sanek, and Sambor, belongs to the Ruthenian Church of Poland, and was united to the Catholic Church. The Metropolitan See of Lemberg was erected for the two millions of Ruthenian Catholics in Gallicia, by Pius VII., in 1807. Kalik and Kameneck being united to it. But besides this many schismatical Slavs in Hungary followed the example set by their Polish brethren in 1595. The union lasted only till 1627, and though a Bishop of Munkacs became Catholic in 1649, the population remained schismatic. More was done for the Catholic cause by the Ruthenian Bishop De Camillis at the end of the 17th century, and in 1771 the diocese of Munkacs was properly constituted by Clement XIV. The Catholic population amounts to 360,000 souls. In Croatia the Ruthenians had one diocese, that of Kreutz, with 20,000 souls, erected in 1777, and subject to the Latin Metropolitan of Agram.

The Ruthenians have a married secular clergy and religious who follow the rule of St. Basil. The bishops are usually taken from the monks. The Ruthenians are under the laws made by Propaganda for Catholics of Greek rite living among Latins. Their bishops at their consecration make the profession of faith prescribed for the Greeks by Urban VIII. The marriage of Ruthenian priests has the same effect as elsewhere— the generation of indifference if not contempt in the people.

## THE ARMENIANS.

The Armenian nation was converted by their great apostle, Gregory the Illuminator, at the beginning of the fourth century. They became schismatics at the close of the sixth century. A union between the Armenians and the orthodox Greeks was effected at a council at Charnum (Erzeroum), in 632, but did not last long. The Armenians held fast to the monophysite doctrine, that in Christ there was but one nature, and external differences increased the opposition between them and the Greeks. They maintained the old Eastern custom of celebrating Christ's birth and his epiphany on one day—January 6th. They were charged by the Greeks with making the priesthood a caste, and only ordaining sons of priests, and, further, with a semi-Jewish practice of cooking flesh in the sanctuary and giving portions of it to the priests.

HEAD OF THE ARMENIAN CHURCH.—The Catholicos, the highest ecclesiastical dignitary, lives at Etchniazin, which has belonged, since 1828, to Russia. He is chosen from the metropolitans by the synod, with the consent of the Armenian bishops and of all Armenians present at the place, and the election must be confirmed by the Czar. It is his office to watch over religion and discipline; he consecrates the chrism for his bishops, which he does only once in seven years, and he can convene a national council. In matters of importance he must consult his synod. He is bishop of Ararat.

The Catholicos is chiefly supported by a poll tax on all adults within his diocese, contributions, stole-fees, etc., from the revenues of the monastery at Etchniazin, and the gifts of pilgrims to the shrine of St. Gregory. There are twelve archbishops and bishops, four vartabeds, (or doctors), 60 monks in priest's orders, and 500 other monks in the great monastery just mentioned. The archbishops, bishops, and archimandrites residing there form his synod. Deputies from the Armenian nation are added to their number at the election of a patriarch.

THE PATRIARCHS.—Next come the patriarchs, who are now almost independent of the Catholicos. The patriarchal sees arose from the constant change of the chief see during the disasters of the nation, and also from the Mongol invasion in the fourteenth century. The Patriarch of Constantinople holds the first rank among patriarchs, and is only inferior in name to the Catholicos. He is chosen by the Armenians, lay as well as clerical, at Constantinople, and gets his berat from the Porte. He can consecrate the holy oil, and can appoint and consecrate metropolitan bishops throughout the Turkish dominions, except at Jerusalem. The

Church property is under his control, but he must administer it with the advice of a synod of 20 lay members, chosen by the Porte. There are three other patriarchs with less power.

The metropolitans, according to the canons, are empowered to consecrate their suffragans and the holy oils, but these rights are now reserved to the Catholicos, or else to the patriarch, and the metropolitans differ from other bishops only by insignia. A monk cannot, except by dispensation, become a bishop, and the bishops are usually chosen from the unmarried vartabeds or doctors. The patriarch may nominate, but usually the bishops are chosen by the clergy and fathers of families.

DIFFERENT CLASSES OF PRIESTS.—The priests are divided into two classes, that of the vartabeds or doctors, who are again subdivided into many grades and who remain unmarried, and the parish priests. The former are far more highly esteemed, and the esteem comes from the fact that they are strict celibates. A staff is the mark of their office, and their chief duty consists in preaching. They live by collections made after the sermon. The ordinary clergy are married. They are drawn from the humbler classes, and trained either by a parish priest or at a monastery.

The Armenians have the same minor orders as the Latins, and like them, they reckon the subdeaconate among the greater orders. A priest is elected by the people, who, however, invariably accept the candidate proposed by the lay administrator of the church property. He must then be approved by the bishop. This and the fact that they usually marry causes them to have no weight in the community and very few have any great respect for them. They live by stole-fees and by offerings at Epiphany and Easter. They also get subsidies from the fund for pious uses. But they are very poor and, generally, have to follow some trade.

ARMENIAN MONKS.—The Armenian monks observe the rule of St. Basil, but their fasts are stricter than those of the Greek religious. They have many monasteries, and at least one large convent of nuns, which is situated on Mount Zion.

The whole number of Armenians is about 3,000,000, of whom about 2,400,000 are in Turkey. About 500,000 are in the Russian Empire.

## ABYSSINIAN CHURCH.

SUPERSTITION RIFE.—The Abyssinian is another schismatical Church whose clergy are married. It became monophysite in the fifth century, following the example of many other Eastern Churches. The Abuna, or head of the Abyssinian Church, is always an Egyptian monk, nominated by the Patriarch of Egypt. As in the Greek Church, the priests can marry only once. Superstition is rife among the Abyssinians, and morals and intellect are at a low ebb.

## COPTIC CHURCH.

THE MONOPYHSITE CHRISTIANS IN EGYPT.— Dioscorus, the Patriarch of Alexandria, was deposed by the Council of Chalcedon, in 451, because he maintained there was only one nature in Christ. Orthodox patriarchs and other officials, ecclesiastical and civil, were sent from Constantinople to Egypt, but the mass of people were fanatically attached to monophysite error. Many fled to upper Egypt or took refuge among the Arabs, and at last, when the occasion came, the Copts betrayed Egypt to the Saracens, who drove Greeks and Romans out of the land and for a time treated the Copts well.

But it was only for a time, and under successive Mohammedan dynasties the Copts were subjected to cruel oppression and had to pay an extortionate price for leave to practise their religion. At present they form about one tenth of the population of the country. They represent the ancient inhabitants of Egypt and celebrate Mass in the old Coptic language. In doctrine they agree on the whole with Catholics, except on the single point which led to their separation from the Church, viz., the two natures of Christ.

ALLOWED TO LIVE WITH THEIR WIVES.—Their supreme head is the monophysite Patriarch of Alexandria, who has great authority and is chosen from the monks. Then come the bishops, priests, deacons, and inferior clergy of the Church. The priests are allowed to live with their wives and, as they receive scarcely any support from the Church, generally pursue an ordinary trade. They are obliged to acquire some knowledge of Coptic, for this, the language of the liturgy, is a dead language, Arabic being the vulgar tongue.

They have four fasting seasons, which they observe with remarkable strictness. The principal peculiarity in their ritual is the administration of the sacrament of Extreme Unction, which they give along with the Sacrament of Penance, to heal the diseases of the soul. They have also a custom of blessing large tanks of water in which people bathe. They have adopted circumcision, probably to satisfy Mohammedan prejudice.

The Egyptian Abbott Andrew went to the Council of Florence to seek reunion for the Monophysites with the Roman Church, but most of the Copts adhere to their heresy. There is, however, a Catholic Vicar-Apostolic of the Coptic rite for the courts of Egypt.

## THE MARONITES.

There has been much dispute on the origin of the name, but the following is probably the true account. Maro, a Syrian monk, contemporary with St. Chrysostom, settled on Mount Lebanon, and after his death a monastery called after him, the Monastery of Saint Maro, was founded between Apamea and Emesa, on the Orontes. A monk belonging to this house and known as John Maro, was named bishop of Botrys, in 676, by Mecarius, Patriarch of Antioch, who was afterwards deposed, as a Monothelite, by the 6th General Council. John Maro thus became the spiritual and temporal head of the Christian population on Mount Lebanon, and contended successfully both against Saracens and Melchites. Partly from the John Maro, who died in 707, partly from St. Maro, the patron of the monastery, the Monothelite Christians on Mount Lebanon were called Maronites. In 1182 a Latin Patriarch of Antioch united them to the Catholic Church.

THE SCHISM HEALED—A schism was caused through Greek influence, and a Maronite patriarch fell away. But the rent was healed in 1216, and ever since the Maronites have been steadfast Catholics. The patriarch is chosen by the bishops, the Pope confirming and sending the pallium. He is subject to Propaganda. He appoints and consecrates the bishops. He also consecrates the Holy Oils and chrisms. His income consists of 100,000 piastres from a poll-tax levied on all adult Maronites, a tax of five piastres each levied from the priests' titles, and a subsidy from bishops and religious houses. The parish priests, usually married, are chosen by the people. There are 300 parishes, 500 secular priests. The parish priest is allowed to till land, and his income consists in offerings of corn, oil, silk, and stole fees.

There are three lower or minor orders, *viz.*, psaltist, reader, and sub-deacon; three greater or higher, deacon, priest, bishop. The tonsure is given before the minor orders. There are three general and several diocesan seminaries, the latter of recent origin. There is also a Maronite College at Rome.

MARONITE EDUCATION—Education is given in Arabic, the vulgar, and in Syriac, the liturgical language, and also, of course, in the theological sciences.

The Maronite religion follows the rule of St. Antony. Down to 1757 there were only two congregations, one of St. Isaias, another of St. Antony. Fourteen monasteries belong to the congregation of St. Isaias, in which there are about 1,000 lay brothers and 600 Fathers. There are seven nunneries of the strict observance. There are also many irregular monasteries and nunneries, where the rule is less strict, and the superior must belong to the founder's family. In one convent of Maronite Nuns a Western rule, that of the Visitation, is observed.

# CHAPTER VIII.

## The Russian Church.

ITS GREAT WEALTH—DIVIDED INTO SECTS—MARRIAGE AMONG ITS CLERGY—A HINDRANCE TO SANCTITY AND ZEAL—PRIESTS LIVING IN LUXURY AND DESPISED BY THE PEOPLE—INCLINED TO PROTESTANTISM.

Gibbon does not hesitate to call the Russians "the most ignorant and most superstitious followers of the Greek communion." Nevertheless, they are a great people with great qualities, but their progress in civilization has been retarded by the schism which has withdrawn them from the humanizing influence of the Roman Pontiff.

Methodius, Archbishop of Twer, published in 1805 an historical work, in Latin, on the first four ages of Christianity, and in it he says that a great portion of the Russian clergy is Calvinist. Notwithstanding the great affinity of doctrines between the Roman and the Greek Churches, yet the Russian studies no other than Protestant books. Philaret, a patriarch of Moscow, a man of talent and cultivated mind, formed a school of theologians imbued with the spirit of Protestantism. He issued a catechism and a review of the controversies between East and West. The Russians know little about Catholic theologians, but read and study Germans like Neander and Schleiermacher, and there is a constant tendency to soften the points between themselves and Protestants, and to accentuate those which separate Russians from Catholics.

The Russian Church was first severed from the Roman in the eleventh century, by the schism of Michael Cærularius. Subsequently it took its religion from Constantinople. While under the Mongolian yoke, several attempts were made to unite again with the Holy See at Rome, but in vain.

POPULATION AND CREEDS.—The total population of all the Russians is nearly 85,000,000. The various creeds of European Russia were estimated, in 1879, as follows :

| | |
|---|---:|
| Greek Orthodox, | 51,835,000 |
| Raskolnics (Schismatics), | 12,000,000 |
| United Greeks and Armenio Gregorians, | 2,950,000 |
| Jews, | 3,000,000 |
| Moslems, | 2,600,000 |
| Pagans, | 26,000 |

In 1881, the number of Greek Orthodox throughout the Empire, excluding two foreign bishoprics, was estimated at 61,941,000.

GREAT WEALTH.—In 1882 there were in Russia 40,569 orthodox churches and about 14,000 chapels, with 37,318 priests, 7009 deacons, and 45,395 singers. There were also 6752 monks, and 3957 aspirants, 4945 nuns, and 13,803 female aspirants. The Church budget was 18,974,887 roubles (about $14,500,000) in 1884. The monasteries and churches are possessed of great wealth, including 2,950 square miles of land (a territory greater than that of Oldenburg) an invested capital of 22,634,000 roubles (about $17,500,000), an annual subsidy of 408,000 roubles (about $320,000) from Government, and a very great number of inns, shops, printing establishments, burial grounds, etc., with whole towns covering an aggregate area of 10½ squares miles. Their total annual revenue is estimated at 9,000,000 roubles (about $7,000,000).

The word Rascolnic in the Russian language signifies literally schismatic. The schism designated by this generical expression originated in the ancient translation of the Bible, to which the Rascolnics cling tenaciously, and which contains texts that, according to them, are altered in the version made use of by the Russian Church. On this ground they call themselves (and who may hinder them?) men of the ancient faith, or old believers (slaroversi). Whenever the people, possessing, unfortunately for themselves, the Holy Scriptures in the vulgar tongue, persist in reading and interpreting them, no aberration of private judgment need astonish. It would be too long to relate in detail the numerous superstitions which have been added to the original grievances of these bewildered men. The sect, soon after its commencement, was divided and subdived, as always happens, to such a degree, that at this moment there are in Russia perhaps forty sects of Rascolnics. All are extravagant, and some abominable. Besides, the Rascolnics protest *en masse* against the Russian Church, as the latter protests against the Roman. The motive, the argument, the right, are the same on both sides, so that any complaint on the part of the prevailing authority would be ridiculous.

NEITHER SHOCKS NOR ALARMS.—Rascolnism neither alarms nor shocks the nation at large, any more than other false religions; the higher classes think of it only to make sport of it. As for the priesthood, it never undertakes anything against the dissenters, because it knows its weakness, and that, moreover, the spirit of proselytizing must be essentially wanting to it. Rascolnism does not extend beyond the ranks of the people; but the people is really something, even if its members amounted only to thirty millions. Men who profess to be well informed already estimate the number of these sectaries at nearly the seventh of the whole people. The government, which alone knows what to think on the matter, says nothing about it, and it does well. It, moreover, treats the Rascolnies with unequalled prudence, moderation, and goodness; and, even although unfortunate consequences should be the result, it would always find consolation in the reflection that severity would not have succeeded better.

Everywhere the clergy are married and without influence. The Nonconformists form a strong body in Russia, and Protestant doctrines are popular among them. The rationalist sects spread in North and West Russia in the fourteenth century, and greatly increased in the sixteenth. They have given rise to various bodies which deny the Divinity of Christ or explain away various dogmas and prescriptions of orthodoxy. "Protestantism," says W. R. Morfill, M. A., "with its more or less rationalistic tendencies, has made itself increasingly felt, especially during the present century, and in Southern Russia." Another tendency pervading the whole of Russian nonconformity is that which seeks a return to communistic principles.

MARRIAGE AND THE SECTS.—All sects deal more or less with the question of marriage and the position of woman. A few of them solve it by encouraging—at least during their "love feasts,"—absolutely free relations between all "brethren and sisters." Nonconformity, which formerly had no hold upon Little Russia, has suddenly begun to make progress there in the shape of the "Stunda," a mixture of Protestant and rationalistic teaching, with tendencies towards a social but rarely socialistic reformation.

The discipline of the Russian Church has undergone many changes. In the Middle Ages the Metropolitan of Russia was nominated by the Duke, and consecrated by the Patriarch of Constantinople. Once consecrated, the Metropolitan had immense power, even in secular matters. The bishops were well supported by tithes, and held secular jurisdiction in their own lands, and no prince could engage in war, until a bishop had given his blessing.

Since the time of Catherine II. (who seized all the Church property) the Russian Church has been supported by the State. Its synod, which consists of twelve members, is nominated by the Czar, and the members removed at will. The Czar is therefore the Pope.

BISHOPS CHOSEN FROM MONKS.—The bishops are all unmarried, and are therefore chosen from among the monks. This proves that there is a glimmering idea that celibacy is the proper state for a clergy. The "white" or secular clergy must all be married, and are mostly sons of priests. They begin their education at the parish school, continue it at the parish school and diocesan seminary, and finish at one of the four ecclesiastical academies. Three or four years are spent at one of these stages. The benefices are all conferred by the bishop, except that landed proprietors have often a right of patronage in country churches.

A canon of the fifteenth century required a priest who lost his wife to live like a layman in a monastery. This law of enforced seclusion was set aside by Peter the Great. A widowed priest may now get leave from the synod to officiate as before ; and even in the case of second marriage, an edict of Peter the Great, in 1724, permits a priest to be employed as rector of a seminary, or in the episcopal chancery, if he has applied himself diligently to study, and especially to preaching.

The Russian religious follow the rule of St. Basil. Men must not be professed till they are forty, and women till they are fifty. The novitiate lasts three years, and is followed by another period of probation. The discipline is strict, and only a few monks receive holy orders. Regular priests never have parishes.

THE POLES RESIST MARRIAGE.—In 1842 it was sought to introduce priestly marriage in Russian Poland. A priest of the day named Taillard strenuously opposed it, and in his arguments affirmed that, if celibacy had not been compulsory in the primitive Church, it ought to have been. " If the celibacy of the priesthood," he said, " be not from the beginning of Christianity, it ought to have been there, for, as our holy religion comes from God, it should contain in itself all the means possible to elevate the nations to the highest point of liberty and happiness."

Father Gagarin, of the Society of Jesus, who has made a thorough investigation into the state of the modern Russian Church, very properly observes that the situation of the Russian clergy is but imperfectly known out of Russia. Protestants do not seek to know because they do not want to know.

PRIESTHOOD A CASTE.—Father Gagarin proves that the priesthood in Russia has become a caste. The son of a priest or deacon is destined from his birth to enter the clerical ranks. It is an obligation from which he is not permitted to withdraw himself. On the other hand the son of a nobleman, merchant, citizen, or peasant who desired to become a priest would meet with insurmountable difficulties.

DAUGHTERS TO BE SETTLED.—Marriage before ordination used to be licensed; finally it became obligatory. "It seems at least," says the French priest, "that the Seminarist, obliged to be married before receiving Holy Orders, must be free to choose his companion. But priests and deacons have daughters for whom settlement must be found; hence arose a prohibition from marrying out of the caste. There are some bishops who do not even tolerate their clergy marrying out of their diocesan clergy. By what right do you impose on the daughter of an ecclesiastic the obligation to become the wife of a priest or of a deacon? The inclination of her heart, social proprieties, the blessing of her parents, cannot these point out to her elsewhere a happy path of life? Why, on his side, should not the son of a priest find a companion in the family of a decent *employé* of one of the lower gentry, of a rich peasant, of a citizen, of a tradesman?"

Another curious thing is that the houses exclusively appropriated to the education of the daughters of ecclesiastics are nothing more than boarding schools to educate daughters to become the wives of priests.

A PRIEST AS A GOOD "MATCH."—"Without speaking of the prescriptions of the Canon Law," says Father Gagarin, "who does not see the very great difference between a married man clothed with the sacerdotal character, and a priest in whom mothers and their daughters might see a *match*, or who himself, among the young people with whom his functions bring him in contact, might look for one to whom he could offer his heart and hand, and pay his courtship? In such a situation, what would become of confession?"

LUXURY.—In 1872 there was published in Leipsic a book, written in the Russian Language, on the White and Black Clergy of Russia. The author shows that the priests were living on the "fat of the land." Speaking of the curés of the principal parishes of the capital, he says:—

"The curés of Petersburg have not to trouble themselves about their dwelling; apartments are gratuitously provided for them, such as could not be rented for less than $800, $1,200, or $1,600 a year. The furniture is drawn from the first shops of Petersburg. Rich carpets cover the floors of the drawing room, study, and chamber; the windows display fine hangings; the walls, valuable pictures. Footmen in livery are not rarely seen in the anteroom. The dinners given by these curés are highly appreciated by the most delicate epicures. Occasionally their *salons* are open for a soirée or a ball; ordinarily it is on the occasion of a wedding, or the birth-day of the curé, or on the patron saint's day. The apartments are then magnificently lighted up; the toilettes of the ladies are dazzling; the dancing is to the music of an orchestra of from seven to ten musicians. At supper the table is spread with delicacies, and champagne flows in streams. A Petersburg curé, recently deceased, loved to relate that at his daughter's nuptials champagne was drunk to the value of 300 roubles ($240)."

GIVES BALLS AND PARTIES.—The same book just quoted from states that in the provinces, though the clerical display is less grand, yet it is greater than is seen in any other profession in the locality. The curé clothes himself in the finest, and his wife and daughters are walking advertisements of the milliner's art. "The reverend gentleman," says the anonymous author, "gives at his parsonage soirées and balls, at the latter of which the daughters of priests dance with the young men of the Seminaries, to the great scandal of the superiors of those institutions!" (*sic.*)

The sympathetic writer goes on to commiserate the country priests, who "are forced to accompany, bareheaded," a dead body to the cemetery, and to "confess rude and ignorant people." Well, confession in the country more than once a year is something almost unheard of.

One of the scandals of the Russian Church is that the penitent, on receiving absolution, by custom gives money to the confessor. In towns this sum frequently rises to $1, $2, and $4, sometimes to much more. In the village the peasant offers only a kopec, about one cent, but on receiving communion he is obliged to renew his offering for prayers before communion, at the moment of communion, after communion, and for having his name enrolled, etc.

SOURCES OF REVENUE.—A source of revenue to the priest are the prayers chanted at home in every house in the parish, many times a year. Often enough, says Father Gagarin, in spite of all the prohibitions of the Synod, the wives and children of the priests, deacons, and clerks accompany their husbands and fathers, and stretch out their hands also. "The worst of all this is that the Russian peasant, while long disputing merely about a few centimes, will think himself insulted unless the priest accept a glass of brandy. And when the circuit of all the houses in the village has to be made, though he stay only a few minutes in each, this last gift is not without its inconveniences."

CHARACTER OF THE PRIESTHOOD.—In a few sentences Father Gagarin pictures the character of the Russian priesthood. Says the French priest:—

"In the Catholic clergy there can exist abuses and disorders; there have been and still are, more or less, according to different countries. Without going far, for example, the joy we feel from the marvelous transformation wrought under our eyes in the German clergy must not make us forget the tears wrung from us 40 or 50 years ago." (He was writing in 1872.) "I admit it; but in spite of that, I do not believe that there is in the Catholic Church, or even in the Protestant Churches, a clergy fallen so low as the Russian, and which answers so little to what we might justly expect it to be. This unhappy clergy appears to have reached the point of self-persuasion that all its duties are fulfilled in chanting the offices. As to making Jesus Christ known and loved, or pointing out to souls the way to tread in his footsteps, it does not even dream of such a thing. The salvation of souls redeemed by Jesus Christ at the price of his own blood concerns it not; its thought goes not beyond a few formalities understood after a Jewish fashion. * * * Where must we look for the root of the evil? In the vicious organization of the clergy; in this obligation of marriage imposed on all the aspirants to the priesthood—an obligation known to the canon law of the East, and which has resulted in making the clergy an hereditary caste."

STUDENTS MADE DRUNK.—In his chapter on the "Black Clergy," Father Gagarin says that ecclesiastical authority uses every means to determine a certain number of academic pupils to embrace the monastic life. He cites an example of a student having been made intoxicated and in that condition receiving the tonsure and making his religious profession.

"The academic pupils," he says, "do not scruple to frequent the cafés, restaurants, and public houses of the neighborhood. There they are sometimes so intoxicated as to lose all consciousness, and are obliged to be carried home to the academy on a hand-barrow. When it is desired to induce one of these students to embrace the religious life spite of his repugnance, they watch that he become in his turn the hero of one of these orgies. The superior is ready to pardon, to forget everything, if the offender give him evidence of a sincere repentance. Of this he accepts but one proof—the signature of the student to a paper containing a request that he be allowed to make his religious profession."

FALSE SWEARING.— Father Gagarin states that many a young man finishes his studies at 25, some at 23, some at 19. According to the law an academy pupil must be 25 before he can pronounce his vows. The religious superiors falsify the age to bring about his profession— they "commit a sin rather than violate an imperial ordinance, which could easily be repealed or dispensed from. But, in their eyes, a ukase is more inviolable than a commandment of God."

Those who do not finish their studies before thirty years of age are left to do as they please. There is no one to guide or counsel them. When they are weary behind the cloister walls there is always the means of exit, with or without permission, by day or night.

As to the bishops in Russia they are mere figure-heads. Of rural authority and influence they have none. Pastoral letters are never heard of, and the discourses they pronounce on solemn occasions no one cares about. As bishops they do not exercise in their plenitude their imprescriptible rights. "They must allow us to say, they are not truly bishops, but mitred functionaries," says the Abbé Jager.

REVEALING SECRETS OF THE CONFESSIONAL.—As a result of this kind of education the Russian clergy have never scrupled to reveal the secrets of the confessional. Nay, the "Spiritual Regulation" commands them to reveal certain things. The 11th and 12th rules say that, if there be a plot against the emperor or the empire, or any machination against the honor or life of the emperor or his majesty's family, and the penitent be unwilling to abandon it, the priest must reveal it. Or, if a false miracle be admitted as true and the author of the imposture come to confess it, without, however, wishing to reveal it, also in that case the confessor is bound to reveal the secret of the confessed and to denounce the guilty.

How different is the practice in the Catholic Church. There have been bad priests, but not one has yet been known to have revealed the secrets of the confessional.

INSULTING TO CHASTITY.—"The "Spiritual Regulation," says the Abbé Gagarin, "prescribes to confessors betrayal, forbids monks the use of the pen, insults the chastity of those virgins who wish to consecrate their virginity to God; it has no bowels of compassion for the poor, and we look in vain for a single word breathing love to God or our neighbor."

If the Eastern Church had maintained the same rigorous rule in regard to celibacy, this degeneracy of morals, as the Rev. Dr. Alzog points out, would not have occurred.

## CHAPTER IX.

### How Protestantism "Reformed."

DEPLORABLE EFFECTS OF LUTHER'S ATTACKS ON CLERICAL CELIBACY—SOCIETY IN GERMANY UPROOTED—A FRIGHTFUL REIGN OF IMMORALITY—WHAT DR. DŒLLINGER SAYS.

Some years ago "Harper's New Monthly Magazine" printed an attack upon the Papacy. The article contained many historical inaccuracies, which have been copied and recently repeated elsewhere. For instance, it asserted that the law of celibacy originated with St. Gregory VII., and gave a fancy sketch of married priests and monks being declared polluted and degraded, showing how they were "branded with shame and ignominy." "Wives," it went on to say, "were torn from their devoted husbands, children were declared bastards, and the ruthless monk, in the face of the fiercest opposition, made celibacy the rule of the Church."

PRETENDED MARRIAGES.—As we have already abundantly proved, the celibacy of the clergy was the law of the Church and of the German Empire, and every priest knew it before taking orders, and so "Harper's" is very much in the wrong. These pretended marriages were, in both the ecclesiastical courts and the civil courts, no marriages at all, and these despairing wives of priests were simply concubines. As Orestes A. Brownson in his answer shows, Gregory did his best to enforce the law which the emperors had suffered to fall into desuetude. It is not claimed that every priest and every bishop in all ages of the Church was without stain. Such an assumption would be absurd. Even in the circle of the apostles which surrounded our Lord Himself there was sin, the gravest, and much of it. There was a Judas Iscariot.

RIGHT OF INVESTITURE.—No, but the Church, as the agent of its Divine Founder, tried to inculcate the precepts imparted to her, and was always thundering in the cause of morality and charity. The right of the investiture of bishops was always in the Pope, and it was only by his authority that the emperors had ever exercised it. "The Pope," says Brownson, "had authorized them to give investiture of bishops at a time of disorder, and it was for the good of the Church that they should be so authorized. But when they abused the trust, and used it only to fill the Sees with creatures of their own, or sold the investitures for money to the unworthy and the profligate, and intruded them into Sees, in violation of the canons, and sheltered them from the discipline of the Church—causing thus gross corruption of morals and of manners, the neglect of religious instruction, and dangers to souls—it was the right and the duty of the Pontiff to revoke the authorization given, to dismiss his unworthy agents, and to forbid the emperors henceforth to give investitures."

REFORMS OF GREGORY THE GREAT.—When Gregory VII. was firmly seated on the throne, he at once set himself to reform the abuses and scandals of the Church, the existence of which he constantly deplored in letters. In one of his letters he said:—

"The Eastern Church has lost the true faith, and is

now assailed on every side by infidels. In whatever direction one turns his eyes—to the West, to the North, or to the South—everywhere are to be found bishops who have obtained the episcopal office in an irregular way; whose lives and conversation are out of harmony with their calling; who go through their duties not for love of Christ, but from motives of worldly ambition. * * * Those among whom I live—Romans, Lombards, and Normans—are, as I have often told them, worse than Jews and pagans."

REVIVING THE OLD DECREES.—Gregory began his work with the reformation of the clergy. He first of all assembled a numerously attended synod at Rome (A. D. 1074), and revived all the old decrees against incontinency—he did not originate, be it observed, he revived decrees already made—and enjoined their observance under the severest penalties. This he considered the only efficient means of restoring and preserving among the clergy the moral purity of life which their state demanded. In no other way could they be so detached from the world and worldly affairs, as to devote themselves wholly to the services of the Church, or be completely independent of the state. Gregory was furiously opposed, but he made the people, in a measure, the executors of his will. Religiously minded men and women would have nothing to do with those priests who refused to yield obedience to the laws of the Church or to strengthen the authority of the Pope.

LUTHER'S "REFORM."—Will Protestants, in the face of these historical facts, persist in asserting that the Popes never made an attempt to reform abuses that had crept into the Church? But what sort of a reformation did the Protestants bring about? Did they improve the morality of their times? Did they make men and women better? Let us see; let us hear the testimony of impartial witnesses.

The founder of the Protestant religion, Martin Luther, even after he had abandoned the faith of his boyhood, did not take the matrimonial step without reluctance. Subsequently he made his doctrine upon the marriage of the clergy conform to the rest of his system. He taught that celibacy, inasmuch as its aim was ascetic, was not only not a divine precept, but was rather in opposition to the divine will. Consequently, he said, any one who made such a vow was a guilty person, and that when such a vow had been made it would and should be broken.

HATERS OF RELIGION.—These principles of the so-called reformation were put into practice by thousands and taught from every Protestant pulpit. Haters of religion had said before Luther that the sensual instinct of man was a power absolutely uncontrollable. Luther taught that it was necessary to obey this power, that it was "a holy act," that no one ought to resist or refuse to obey a requirement as great as eating, or drinking, or waking, or sleeping, that, God having said "Increase and multiply," therefore no one had been created to live in continence, and that perfect chastity was utterly impossible, unless God should perform a miracle.

INCREASE AND MULTIPLY.—It is scarcely necessary to pause to point out that the injunction of the Almighty, "increase and multiply," was given to the animals, the lower orders of creation, and not to man. But we must call particular attention to this remarkable utterance of the founder of Protestantism, and the advocate of priestly marriage:—

"To be without a wife and to make a vow of chastity, while God does not see fit to perform a miracle, is just as if one had made a vow to commit adultery or to break in some other way the divine law. Whosoever does not contract marriage cannot but fall into licentiousness; how can it be otherwise?"

Dr. Dœllinger on the Right Side.—Some years ago Protestantism thought it was about to get a chance to quote the learned Dr. Döllinger against the Church. The distinguished German, however, did not go to the length the enemies of the Pope thought he would. But we can quote Dr. Döllinger against the above passage from Luther. In his work on the Reformation and its results he comments in this passage:—

"Therefore," says Dr. Döllinger, "Luther asserts that not to take a wife is an infraction of the divine law greater than committing adultery, robbery, or some other crime of that kind, that a person with all his faculties who did not wed would incur the divine anger, and (horrible to say) in the case of an individual upon a bed of sickness, he was obliged to make at least a firm resolution to marry, if possible, before he breathed his last. Luther adds that a man cannot, without sinning, be estranged from woman; that, as a general rule, we cannot resist nature; that, whatever we do, nature must have her way; that to bind one self by oath to be barren, not to have children, is as if the sun had made a vow not to give light. * * * There is one thing worthy of remark, which is that the works in which Luther has given himself the most latitude on this subject are precisely those which he has composed for the people, and so the effects of his principles are felt more widely than doubtlessly he had thought, and probably this did not enter into his calculations.

Influence of Luther's Teachings.—"The influence of his declarations, daily and rapidly propagated, was not exercised alone upon the secular clergy, upon the monks and the nuns, (but comparatively less upon the latter); it made itself felt upon that class, then as in our day, the most numerous, the members of which, through their peculiar way of living, their calling, their poverty, or other social circumstances, were not in a condition to marry and bring up a family, or who, at least, could not do so until well advanced in years, and who consequently passed the best years of their youth and their strength in enforced celibacy. These began to learn for their first time that this continent life, which until then had been required of them, was altogether an impossibility, and that to resist the impulses of nature was not only beyond their power, but a species of rebellion against the decrees of Providence. They saw in the new society everybody who had been bound by vows, even by vows freely made, making it a duty, following the example of the Reformers, to violate their vows in the face of the world, as if they were not and could not be valid, because, they alleged, one could not bind himself to do what was impossible, and could not be bound by a promise contrary to the eternal laws of nature. They were given innumerable pamphlets; they daily listened to sermons in which the state of virginity and the superiority of a life vowed to chastity were not only combated and rejected, but even treated with ridicule and extravagance. They saw, in one word, how the principle of the impossibility of chastity, once admitted, had a solvent action even upon the bonds of matrimony.

"We can understand, without much trouble, that in a time of general excitement, where all kinds of means are employed to excite and entertain suspicion of the doctrine and discipline of the ancient Church, such a spectacle should have had a deep and lasting effect upon souls."

CITING AUTHORITIES—Dr. Döllinger gives examples of the evil effects of the teachings of Luther and his followers on this subject, and cites authorities:—*
"Another member of the university-body, the Rector Conrad Klauser of Zürich, said in 1554 that, in consequence of the implacable war waged against celibacy in Protestant society, people had come to attach not the least importance to continency and chastity."

LIKE PAGAN ROME—This is very much like the state of Roman society when Christianity was first preached, and which, as we have shown elsewhere, the Roman writers in general, and satirists in particular, have pictured! Well, history repeats itself in every case. Where there are no religious restraints, mankind is deeply sunk in sin.

Dr. Döllinger continues:—" It were preferable, without doubt, wrote Mathias Schenck, Rector of Augsburg, to Jerome Wolf, in 1571, if men who had devoted themselves to the cultivation of the sciences were to live in celibacy; unfortunately, we have seen for a number of years past the opinion prevail that it is impossible for man to live a chaste life. What God said to our first parent—that it is not good for man to live alone—is applied now, without exception, and to the great detriment of the public welfare, to all circumstances, and to all individuals who have attained the age of puberty, so that to-day any one who does not marry is looked upon but as a violator of the divine law." (Amœnitates litterariæ, x. 1075).

YOUTH HORRIBLY CORRUPTED.—He quotes Conrad

* (Clauserus, de Educatione Puerorum. Basileæ, 1554, p. 76).

Porta as saying, in 1580, that formerly young virgins used to give themselves up to maceration and mortification the most severe, but that in the new state of society young girls were more remarkable for impatience, shamelessness, and lewdness; clandestine and guilty meetings had become so common that people hardly regarded them as reprehensible; that boys and girls conducted themselves with the greatest licence; that generally people married to be able the more freely to give themselves up to their passions, and that a great number, after having appropriated the property of others, "took to their heels" and conducted themselves, under the guise of marriage, like Bohemians and Turks. (Porta, Jungfrauen-Spiegel; f. 1 et seq., 95, 225.)

EVERYBODY WANTING TO WED.—"The want of circumspection," says Dr. Döllinger, "and the rapid spread of lust, of shamelessness, of libertinism, and of adultery, were in the very first days of the Reformation subjects for lament on the part of German reformers. 'Scarcely have the young men of to-day,' said Brenz in 1532, (Brentii homiliæ, xxii., D.), 'divested themselves of their swaddling clothes, than they want to take a wife. Girls who are not yet marriageable expect husbands, and priests, monks, nuns marry in violation of all human laws.' Four years before, the 'reformer' of the city of Ulm, Conrad Sam, had complained of the spread of debauchery, of the great number of adulteries, of the corrupt influence which was at work, and of the bragging way in which people seemed to talk of their wickedness. (Christliche Unterweisung der Jungen, etc., gepredigt zu Ulm in der Pfarr im 1528, D. 8.).

MARRIAGE LIGHTLY TREATED.—"In 1539 Bugenhagen (Bugenhagen, von Ehesachen, vom Ehebruch und heimlichen Weglaufen, Wittenberg 1540, R. 2, 4; von mancherlei christ. Sachen, i., 455.) said:—' Do you not see with what levity they treat marriage and how wicked men make light of bringing dishonor into families and laughingly say they are 'gallants,' 'lucky,' 'welcome to ladies?' * * * Link, a colleague of Osiander, (1537) confessed that in his time so little importance was attached to impurity that everywhere it was the subject for joking."

In a note Dr. Döllinger says:—" In other passages Luther comes very near approving of polygamy. 'It is not written,' said he, 'that man shall not have more than one wife. If it is a question for men to pronounce upon, then I would not condemn now, nor yet would I advise it.' But in his table talk he declares that concubinage is a true marriage before God, by no means prejudicial although scandalous."

LUTHER REPROVED.—George, Duke of Saxony, reproached the reformer of Wittenberg, in 1526, in the following manner:—

" When did we see wives leave their husbands and give themselves up to others, as we see them, under your gospel, do now? When was adultery as common since you advised and wrote this:—' Let a wife who is barren with her husband take to another man, that she may have children to rear and *vice versâ*'? What a gospel have you boasted of having given to the world!" (Edit. de Jena, 1556, iii., 211.)

NUMBERLESS SOULS LOST.—Dr. Döllinger quotes Wizel as follows, (Evangelium Luthers, D. 4);—" Truly, Luther has done so well by his preaching that we have come to regard it as impossible to live and work out our salvation without marriage, yet this new prophet having been the cause of so many foolish unions, of the dissolution of a great many others, of the increase of women of ill-fame and of men leading bad lives, recants and chides his preachers, instead of rewarding them for the energy with which they have propagated his doctrine. What is the use of long phrases? He has expressed himself with so much grossness and immodesty upon this delicate subject, that many souls have been lost, the like of which has never yet been seen. Through his attacks and his steady incitements numbers of poor monks and unfortunate nuns have broken their vows and married and are to-day sunk in the depths of remorse, while he cares not so long as his own wants are satisfied."

"PROTESTANT DEMORALIZATION."—"The facts," says Dr. Döllinger, "bear out the assertions of Wizel upon the natural effects of the doctrine of Luther. When, thirty years later, Sylvester Ezecanovius published the result of his observations upon the state of morality in the two Churches, in the papal Church and 'in the Evangelical,' he also confirms all that had been said before him upon Protestant demoralization, and expressly lays the greater part of the responsibility upon this very doctrine of the leader of the Reformation. Whilst marriage was considered a sacrament, modesty and morality reigned in the family; but when people read in the books of Luther that marriage was a human invention, and in those of Melanchthon that it was foolish, a human trifle, these principles have been put into practice, and to-day marriage is more honored and more decent among the Turks than among the Evangelicals of Germany."

A SHAMEFUL PRACTICE.—"Will any one tell me," says Ezecanovius, "after having read the statements of history, if he has seen in any age the dissolution of marriage more shamefully advocated, and in more forms, than in the age in which we live? Assuredly not, never has been seen such libertinism. We cannot but be astonished when we see, as is the case among us, this strange maxim of Luther set forth as a divine law—that man can no more live in continence than he can abstain from expectorating, and that he is as much bound to take a wife as to eat and drink. It was Nero, the Pagan, Nero, the tyrant, who was the first to hoist the standard of incontinence, and who, from the depths of infamous voluptuousness into which he had plunged, decreed the impossibility of youth and maiden, man or woman, if they were perfect beings, not following the sexual instinct.

It was Nero's Principle.—"This principle of Nero was revived by Luther and propagated by him throughout Germany, and all who eat, drink, and feel the spur of animal passions shamelessly hasten to place themselves under his banner. Young people are no longer afraid to live openly in lewdness;—would you withdraw them from that sink of iniquity? Then they cry out lustily for marriage, they demand that you give them a wife. And the young women, when they have fallen, or in some way led a vicious life, they know, as well as the young men, how to entrench themselves behind the Neronian law of Luther, that tyrant, who, judging others by himself, declared that chastity was impossible to man, and that indulging the sensual appetite was just as imperious and exacting as the necessity to renew our strength by eating and drinking. In accordance with these new views of marriage we see to-day mere boys and girls thus allying themselves."

Degenerate Children.—Then Ezecanovius remarked sarcastically:—

"And from such unions are to spring those great

heroes who are destined, by force of arms, to chase the Turk back beyond the Caucasus, to give us an assurance of peace through their wise counsels, and without doubt to make the rest of Christendom participate in that golden age to which Germany is beholden for her splendor! Truly this new theory of marriage justifies the Evangelicals in saying of themselves: ' *We* are born old men, whilst the Italians, the Spaniards, and the Portuguese are always young.'" (Sylvester Ezecanovius, de corruptis Moribus utriusque partis, Pontificiorum videlicet et Evangelicorum, s. l. et a. F. 3 seq.)

MINISTERS COMPARED WITH PRIESTS.—Ministers, he adds, were not exempt from the general depravity. If the ministers had not greater facilities for concealing their backslidings than the Catholic prelates, (to whom others were constantly turning their attention, whilst nobody else thought it worth while to take notice of these heretics) we would see the marriage tie among the greater part of them, as well as among the bishops, broken. He relates the testimony of those who had inspected the Lutheran Churches. These people had told him that they had come across a greater number of shameful actions and of instances of adultery among the Lutheran clergy than they had ever found in the same space of time among the Catholics. The divorce cases, continues Ezecanovious, had become so common among the Evangelicals, that there could be no doubt that the false interpretation of the words of St. Paul— "But if they cannot contain, let them marry, for it is better to marry than to burn," (I. Cor. vii., 9)—had already worked great harm.

The disorders which the doctrine of Luther had brought about in matrimonial matters were precisely those, says Dr. Döllinger, which served as an argument to Protestant theologians to demonstrate the necessity of rendering the dissolution of the conjugal tie easier. Bucer in 1531 reproached Catholics with the hardships of their law, which refused to the separated husband or wife the right of contracting new ties.

"How could God," said he, "refuse to his believers, to the servants of grace, what formerly it was not difficult to withhold from the legal slave. Where is the clear-sighted, truthful man who does not know that to-day the matrimonial tie is generally more relaxed than it ever was among the Jews, so that those unions among us are rather ties of torture than true marriages."

Bucer's colleague, Sebastian Meier, was very much afraid that, instead of the repugnance manifested by the Catholics, the Protestants would admit divorce.

Bacili Monner, a Saxon councillor, in 1561 exhorted the magistrates not to proceed in matrimonial affairs with so much levity and want of foresight, remarking that it was easy to see the embarrassment and the demoralization that were flowing from this arbitrary and imprudent way of acting, at a time, too, when men were already too much inclined to permit themselves to be carried away by their passions. The same author adds that never had there been seen so many separated wives as in that fast living century, and that youth ran the greatest risk of being perverted by those dissolute and thoughtless persons, who not only sustained in private conversations, but even taught publicly, the lawfulness and the necessity of the plurality of wives. Who cannot see the result of such doctrines, at a time, above all, when the most extreme demoralization reigned in a fallen world, struck with insanity. It is this which compromises so much the reputation of Protestants in the eyes of their adversaries, who contend that the

Lutheran doctrine serves but to render people more dissolute and intractable, and gives occasion for the scorn of every civil law and of every duty. "These are the great scandals," says Monner finally, "to be deplored by every truly pious person."

# CHAPTER X.

## The Married Minister.

CONTRASTED WITH THE CELIBATE PRIEST—CHRIST ONLY IS THE CATHOLIC'S SPOUSE—RISKS OF THE PROTESTANT CLERGYMAN—HIS FOLLIES AND HIS LUXURIOUS LIFE IN ENGLAND.

"In the regeneration," says Orestes A. Brownson, "what may be called the order of the end, which is promised by the Incarnation, and in which creation is completed and man finds his supreme good by being supernaturally united to the supreme good itself, the paternal and filial relations are spiritual, but no less real, than in the order of generation commencing with Adam. Our spiritual fathers are no less real fathers than our fathers after the flesh. Priests are called fathers, and really are so, and as fathers of our spiritual life they are fathers of a higher order and in a higher sense than our natural fathers, as much higher as the life of the soul is above the life of the body.

LIKE BIGAMY.—" Perhaps in this fact is at least one of the reasons why the Church insists on the celibacy of the clergy and regards with no favor a married clergy, even when she allows priests, married before receiving Holy Orders, to retain their wives. There would be a sort of bigamy in it, for the priest is wedded to the Church, his true spouse, and our spiritual mother. The new birth is as really a birth as natural birth, and the priest married in the natural order seems to be a priest of the order of Adam, rather than a priest of the order of Melchisedech. The spiriritual father owes all his love, all his care and tenderness to his spiritual children, and ought not to be burdened with children after the flesh."

HE IS A SPIRITUAL BRIDE.—They who object to the celibacy of the clergy may find here an answer to their objections. The priest is not really a celibate, he has a spiritual bride and spiritual children, which develop all the higher and nobler qualities of the husband and father. Nor are those virgins who reject marriage after the flesh, and take the vow of chastity, less really wives and mothers than are wives and mothers in the natural order. They are really espoused in the spiritual order, and of each of them it may be said, in the language of Scripture, " Thy Maker is thy husband."

AN EFFICIENT AND POWERFUL AGENT.—From the earliest times the greatest importance was attached by the Church to the priestly office, and an exalted idea was entertained of its character. This can be seen from the care and formality with which the election and ordination of the higher orders of the clergy were conducted, as well as from the practice of celibacy. Celibacy was always regarded by the Church as the most efficient and powerful engine for good, and as conferring a character the most holy and sublime. "The fundamental idea of the priesthood," says the Rev. Dr. John Alzog, professor of Theology at the University of Freiburg, "is that of representatives of Christ, the second and spiritual Adam, whose work they continue, and in whose unmarried state they early recognized the prototype and pattern of their own."

EVEN THE PAGANS.—As we have pointed out elsewhere, even the Pagans could not conceive of a perfect priesthood without the accompanying state of virginity. The honor and reverence paid to the Vestal virgins and sibyls are examples of this universal feeling, and another, perhaps still more striking, was the rule prescribed to the high-priest of the Eleusinian mysteries forbidding him to enter into the marriage state after he had assumed his office, or, if already married, enjoining abstinence from all intercourse with his wife. We have seen that the Jewish priests were also forbidden to have intercourse while engaged in their ministrations at the temple.

ALL IN THREE REASONS.—What more need be said for the practice of clerical celibacy than is said in the following three reasons:—

1.—It is fitting that he who would worthily celebrate the Holy Sacrament of the Mass, an office destined to continue till the end of time, should be distinguished by eminent purity of body.

2.—No one, who does not enjoy this freedom, can give his life undivided to Christ and his Church, and labor with the single purpose of advancing his interests and glory, since the married state necessarily implies a divided heart and pursuits directed to other ends.

3.—The married state would limit that absolute independence so necessary to the successful ministry of the priest.

OF COURSE, ONLY HUMAN.—"The priest ought to marry, because he is only human," says the Protestant. Of course he is only human, but so is the soldier who runs away from the field on the morning of battle. The cowardly soldier has disgraced his flag, and will be punished and at least ignominiously expelled from the army, should he escape the death-sentence.

The Catholic priest who should marry would "disgrace his cloth," and would be expelled from his order. How many thousands of men and women in the world have lived to the mortal end lives of perfect continence? They have gone about their daily avocations, have mingled with friends, companions, and associates, and yet retained their virginity. Why, then, cannot one small class of men, (for the priesthood is only a very small fraction of the population) specially devoted to the service of God, also live continent lives, live just as chastely as those exposed to all the temptations of the world?

A VOLUNTARY VOW. — Yes, the priest is only human, but recollect he has not been forced into holy orders. His act of consecrating himself to the service of the altar is entirely voluntary. He must serve several years of probation, he is daily reminded of the great responsibility he is about to undertake, he is made to prove himself, and finally he is not ordained until he is 25 years of age. Before he arrives at that stage the theological student knows whether he is fitted for the life before him.

But so is the Protestant minister "only human." We may say, without any reflection upon the body in general, that he is too human for his office. He believes in clerical marriage, it is encouraged by his superiors. While he is a theological student there is no rule forbidding his writing to a young lady. And is it not very human to prefer the society of the young lady to the society of the hard, dry books he must study? He must divide his time between the two, and it is "only human" nature, should the studies suffer in that divided allegiance.

STILL FANCY FREE. — Well, he may have safely

tided over his seminary days and have been ordained, still "fancy free." He obtains a curacy, and if good looking and with good prospects, becomes a matrimonial problem to the ladies of his parish. He is not hedged around with that reverence peculiar to the Catholic priest, which makes the Catholic man or woman instinctively feel that the priest is his or her superior, no matter how lowly his birth, or how poor his attainments. But in the case of the young minister there is always the probability of "match-making" going on among mothers with marriageable daughters.

No matter how great the zeal with which the young man has entered upon his duties, he will soon see that it is impossible for him to realize his religious hopes because of the social engagements he is forced to enter into and the peculiar light in which he is regarded by the females of his parish while he is a bachelor.

LOVE COMES AT LAST. — He is only human, and love conquers him sooner or later. Even a monarch courting a maid is not a very dignified picture. The lover is always the subject of jest:—

> The lover, all as frantic,
> Sees Helen's beauty in a brow of Egypt.
>   \*   \*   \*   \*
> And then the lover,
> Sighing like a furnace, with a woful ballad,
> Made to his mistress' eyebrow.
>   \*   \*   \*   \*
> Heaven first taught letters for some wretch's aid,
> Some banished lover or some captive maid.

The power of love is proverbial. The poets (and they know something about that tenderness of the heart called love) tell us in smoothest verse that everything goes by the board for that passion. Our curate or our rector is "only human," and he becomes the subject, naturally, (mayhap the slave) of woman.

> Alas! the love of women, it is known
> To be a lovely and a fearful thing.

"NOT WISELY, BUT TOO WELL."—And then, again, our young clergyman may love "not wisely, but too well"—for he is "only human." The object of his affection may be frivolous, and some act of thoughtlessness on her part may give rise to gossip which, in the case of any other than the *fiancée* of a minister, would pass unheeded. The slightest untoward act may compromise his position and impair his usefulness. Moreover, the language of love is peculiar. It has not the precision and relevancy of words in the ordinary course of business, friendship, political or literary affairs. It is apt to be exaggerated, and though sound in its premises yet false in its conclusions. The cynical observer, who occasionally stumbles across a truth, has said that the language of love is akin to the utterances of insanity. Men and women who have probably devoted the whole or a large portion of their lives to the study of this subject, have authoritatively declared that, under those circumstances, man is not quite responsible for his actions.

NOT A SEMINARY STUDY.—His training in the theological seminary has not fitted him for an event of this character. He has not been taught how to conduct himself under these peculiar circumstances. There are no text books of which he could avail himself, and though his professors may have been through a course of love and have had a profound knowledge of the subject, yet they have not imparted to the student the secrets which experience has taught them. It was not in the curriculum. Therefore our young clergyman has no rules by which he can guide his conduct, or govern his language. Naturally he will speak from the heart, and the intellect will have nothing to do with it. Imagine this young rector, after pouring into the ear of his *fiancée* a torrent of platitudes and " soft nothings," mounting the pulpit and declaiming on the vanities of the world, or going (if he can find the time from his love making) into the house of one of his parishioners to regulate the conduct of the male or female portion of the household. Would not the men listen with a cynical smile to his exhortations, and the women with significant nudges and glances?

" The minister's in love" is the word that goes the round of the parish, and when his " flock " meet him, it is with a peculiar smile. To be sure, there is no law, civil or ecclesiastical, forbidding his falling in love. So far, he is free to follow the inclinations of mind and heart. But who cannot see that the force of his ministrations is much weakened.

AFTER THE " HONEYMOON."—But when he has safely tided over the season of courtship and is at last landed on the shores of matrimony he is compelled to devote a large portion of his time to the study of the character, and perhaps the needs, of his wife. If he has money enough he is bound to follow the fashion of the honeymoon and exile himself from his pastoral work for a month at least. When he has returned and his wife proves that she is all she should be, well and good; but if she should fall short of the standard, what then? Marriage, it is said, is a lottery. He may have drawn a blank. The woman he has chosen may have been totally unfitted, by nature and education, for the position of a minister's wife. In any other sphere her characteristics might pass without comment, or be such as to adorn the ball-room, the drawing room, or the dinner table. But as the Pastor's wife, she may be unsympathetic, a gossip, inclined to frivolity, and thoughtless in making acquaintances. Would not her husband's parishioners say, in answer to his exhortations and animadversions, "Brother, first take the beam out of thine own eye?" He might continue to preserve the respect of his people, but their reverence he would never have. If the minister of religion cannot inspire reverence his usefulness is *nil.*

CHILDREN AND POVERTY.—Then children come, and by and by the house is filled with them. It means increased expense without increase of income. What would support two in ease and comfort would be sadly deficient for four, or six, or eight. The children have to be clothed, and fed, and educated, and "genteel poverty" is the pastor's unhappy lot. Perhaps he may resort to the pen to eke out a living, and then what becomes of the precious souls entrusted to his charge? Still further is lessened the time he can devote to their "spiritual needs." Practically, they are sheep without a shepherd. There is another consideration. Some one of his children, for want of sufficient watchfulness on the father's part, may finally go astray. How great is the discredit thrown on the ministry, for the world will always hold the parent responsible for the wrongdoing of the child. And the same world will joke about it, and will insolently and brutally say: "They are all alike—these parsons and parson's sons are no better than other people." The good man will suffer far more keenly than if he were a layman; but so, too, and in another sense, will the people he had pledged himself to guide, to comfort, and console. Ah! in how much greater need does he himself stand of comfort and of consolation. If the spirit be weak, if the soul be too easily clouded by misfortune, the man who had started out in the heyday of youth, full of bright hopes, and with a determination to do good to his fellow-men, may fall back mentally and spiritually exhausted, and suffer those nearest and dearest to him to follow in the footsteps of that one black sheep.

The Minister's Son—a Tragedy.—This is no fancy picture. The original, the reality, has often been seen in the civil and criminal courts of every Protestant country. The impartial newspaper contains the records. The writer, only a few years ago, in this city of New York, looked upon the bloody corpses of a pair whose lives were sinful, and whose death was one of the most tragic occurrences the city had ever known. An old clergyman, who had spent many years of usefulness in a Connecticut parish, had procured for one of his sons a clerkship in a well-known firm in New York. The young man fell beneath the spell of a woman who had once been a famous beauty in the South. They went and lived together as man and wife for a time. One morning they were both found dead in their lodgings. The young man had shot her, putting a bullet through her head, and then one through his own.

A Life full of Crime.—The investigation which the press made revealed a romantic story full of crime. The woman was twice the young man's age. She was living a double life. Not many blocks away lived her children by a former marriage, all grown up and all thoroughly respectable. Many a year ago her waywardness had brought ruin to her husband—a man of talent and position in the South. She left him, and murder and other crimes marked her subsequent career, till at last retribution overtook her in a terrible shape. For days and days the papers were full of stories of her sinful life.

And that aged clergyman—after viewing the remains of his son, a murderer and suicide—returned to his country parish, broken down in spirit and body, and what little energy he had left was utilized in the care of the wife and mother prostrated by the recollection of her son's terrible end.

SATIRE AND RIDICULE KILL.— Other cases might be cited where the sins of the children have fallen heavily upon the father, and where his usefulness as a minister has in consequence been utterly destroyed. The evil is not confined to the parish alone—the daily press spreads it broadcast. The newspaper is quicker to pounce upon a bad scandal than a good sermon. There is nothing so fatal to any institution as satire and ridicule. These clerical scandals the press invariably treats satirically. It should not be so, for sin is always sad.

FOR EXAMPLE. —Out of innumerable instances of the way in which the daily journal treats these unfortunate affairs we will select one. It was published in a leading New York newspaper on February 6th, 1888. The story helps to point the moral that, if clerical celibacy prevailed in that minister's Church, the scandal never would have arisen. The report is as follows:—

"TURNED FROM HOME IN A STORM.

"HOW A DOMINIE PUNISHED A YOUNG WOMAN WHO WAS NAUGHTY.

"Dominie Bruen, pastor of the fashionable First Presbyterian Church, of Belvidere, N. J., is undoubtedly a pious man—stern, rigid, and orthodox, with a holy horror of sin and naughtiness. But just now he is having a bit of a tussle with his conscience, because he did not allow mercy to season justice, and a young woman is in consequence reaping a very heavy punishment for her peccadilloes.

"The Rev. Dr. Bruen married a wife three weeks ago, and fitted up a very fine home in the select part of the town. Then he secured a companion for his bride; she was a pretty, well educated, and refined young woman, and the dominie's ideal of a model companion. As a matter of course, the young bloods of the town recognized her charms and worshipped them. The swellest of the dudes became deeply enamored, paid her every attention, and the war horses among the gossips of the village scented an engagement.

"Everything went like a pastoral; the household of the dominie was serene and blissful, and his bride was fond of her companion.

### NOT SUCH A JEWEL.

"But when the Rev. Dr. Bruen and his wife returned home from prayer meeting a week ago Saturday night and found the house in great disorder, as though a high old time had made merry in their absence, they marvelled greatly and grew suspicious. The dominie said nothing but kept his eye skinned.

"Then on Tuesday night the dominie woke with a start and trembled. He heard heavy footfalls in the hallways. 'Burglars,' he said, and he pulled on his trousers and with a grim smile took down his shotgun, lit a lantern, and went out into the storm to hunt them. He hunted over the ground as far as the depot, but didn't get a shot at his game.

"The next night he put up a job on the girl, for he

had begun to suspect her of being naughty. The dominie borrowed guile of the devil and started out with his wife, ostensibly to go to church. They walked about the town for awhile and came back. A bright light was burning on the top floor of the house. The dominie sent his wife up the back stairs, and he himself went up the front stairs and rapped on the door of the girl's room. There was a skurrying, but no response. He rapped again, and in a plaintive voice the young woman said that she was getting ready to go to bed and he couldn't come in. But the good dominie insisted and the door was opened.

"The fair maiden had told the truth and was in tears over the intrusion. The dominie asked her what mischief she was up to. Opening a wardrobe door he found his answer. He shut the door and told his wife, who had just come up stairs, to go down.

"Then he opened the door again and brought out by the ear a young man. It was the swellest of dudes.

"'John,' said the dominie, 'I never suspected you of anything like this.' And when John had owned up he added, 'If you will marry her I will perform the ceremony and nobody will know anything about it.'

"'All right,' said John, meekly, and he went home, and has stayed there ever since.

### OUT INTO THE STORM.

"The dominie told his wife that the young woman had been naughty, and then sat in his study and thought it all over. He was filled with a righteous wrath that such 'goings on,' had happened in his house.

"He finally ordered the girl out of his house, despite the protest of his wife. The girl dressed herself lightly and went out. It was snowing heavily, and she was fairly lost to know what to do. Finally she hired a team to take her to her married sister at Belvidere Corners, a few miles away. The drifts were so deep two miles from the town that the driver could go no further. But the girl would not go back, and she started to walk on in the midnight storm.

"She was found unconscious in the snow by Farmer John Landermann, as he was driving to town in the morning, and taken to his home. He and his wife, after two hours' labor, resuscitated her. Her feet were frostbitten and she was in a deplorable condition. She told her story and was nursed till Friday, when she was able to go to her sister's, where she now is in seclusion.

"The Rev. Dr. Bruen refuses to discuss the matter, but 'John' says he is willing to marry the girl and that he had asked her to be his wife, but that she had declined."

A PECULIAR PROTESTANT ARGUMENT.—When the cholera raged fifty or sixty years ago in England and Ireland, a comparison was drawn between the zeal of the Catholic priest and the negligence of the Protestant minister. The minister fled from the sick, the priest succored them. The Protestant Archbishop of Dublin undertook to justify the conduct of his clergy, and set himself to prove the futility of religious succor to the dying. He stated that the ministers who did not go to the bedside of the sick did not fail in their duty, and that the sick who should send for the clergyman did fail in duty. He argued that the sick were bound in conscience not to expose the minister to the danger of contagion. He told his clergy to inculcate upon their people "this essential principle of the Protestant religion"—that whatever "a Christian minister" might do for those "who are approaching their end," was inefficacious, for the sick man was "no longer capable of serving and pleasing God." This very curious document of the Protestant Archbishop may be seen in "The Annals of Christian Philosophy," August, 1832, vol. V., page 156.

DEGRADED THE PRIESTLY DIGNITY.—"Protestantism," said Professor Markheimer, of Heidelberg, "has no less degraded the priestly dignity. To be as little like the Catholic hierarchy as possible Protestant ministers have divested themselves of all religious appearance, and they have very humbly placed themselves at the feet of the temporal power. What the state used to give to *ecclesiastics* is now given to the *laity*. With their priestly vestments the ministers have put off their sacred character. The state has made it a business, and all the evil ought to be put at the door of the Protestant clergy. Soon priests will be no more than ordinary citizens."

# CHAPTER XI.

## Family, Property, and Simony.

A Great Moral Question as it Appears in England—Married Ministers Fly from the Sick—Providing for one's Relatives—Sacking the Monasteries — The Malthusian Theory—The Protestant Church Hated by the Masses.

As a proper sequel to the preceding chapter, let us consider still further the effects of a married clergy, as we see them in a great Protestant country like England. Our authority shall be a member of the "Anglican Church,"—Mr. William Cobbett, British member of Parliament, who was born and bred a Protestant. From his "History of the Protestant Reformation," written years ago, we take the extracts following.

But first we call attention to the fact that every Church has some kind of property belonging to it. This property, real or personal, is given in trust to the clergy. Now, it is a risky thing for the married clergy to undertake to manage this property. There is the danger that they or their offspring may misappropriate it. It was well recognized in the days of Gerson that the temporalities of the Church could only be entrusted to men cut off from family ties.

"You have, without doubt," says Mr. Cobbett, at pages 55 and 56, "fresh in your recollection all the censures, sarcasms, and ridicule, which we have, from our very infancy, heard against the monastic life; what drones the monks, and friars, and nuns were; how uselessly they lived; how much they consumed to no good purpose whatever; and particularly, how ridiculous and even how wicked it was to compel men and women to live unmarried, to lead a life of celibacy, and thus either to deprive them of a great natural pleasure, or to expose them to the double sin of breach of chastity and breach of oath.

ABOLISHING THE MONASTERIES.—" Now this is a very important matter. It is a great moral question; and therefore we ought to endeavor to settle this question, to make up our minds completely upon it, before we proceed any further. The monastic state necessarily was accompanied with vows of celibacy; and therefore it is, before we give an account of the putting down of these institutions in England, necessary to speak of the tendency and, indeed, of the natural and inevitable consequences of those vows.

"It has been represented as unnatural to compel men and women to live in the unmarried state, and as tending to produce propensities to which it is hardly proper even to allude. Now, in the first place, have we heard of late days of any propensities of this sort? And, if we have, have those clergymen and bishops been Catholics, or have they been Protestants? The answer which every one now living in England and Ireland can instantly give to these questions disposes of this objection to vows of celibacy. In the next place, the Catholic Church *compels* nobody to make such vow. It only says that it will admit no one to be a priest, monk, friar, or nun, who rejects such vow. Saint Paul strongly recommends to all Christian teachers an unmarried life. The Church has founded a rule on this recommendation, and that, too, for the same reason that the recommendation was given; namely, that those who have flocks to watch over, or, in the language of our own Protestant Church, who have the care of souls, should have as few other cares as possible, and should by all means be free from those incessant and sometimes racking cares which are inseparable from a wife and family.

His Flock Ignored.—" What priest, who has a wife and family, will not think more about them than about his flock? Will he, when any part of that family is in distress, from illness or other causes, be wholly devoted, body and mind, to his flock? Will he be as ready to give alms, or aid of any sort to the poor, as he would be, if he had no family to provide for? Will he never be tempted to swerve from his duty, in order to provide patronage for sons, and for the husbands of daughters? Will he always as boldly stand up and reprove the Law and the Squire for his oppressions and vices, as he would do if he had no son for whom to get a benefice, a commission, or a sinecure? Will his wife never have her partialities, her tattlings, her bickerings, amongst his flock, and never on any account induce him to act towards any part of that flock, contrary to the strict dictates of his sacred duty?

" And to omit hundreds, yes hundreds of reasons that might, in addition, be suggested, will the married priest be as ready as the unmarried one to appear at the bedside of sickness and contagion? Here it is, that the calls on him are most imperative, and here it is that the married priest will, and with nature on his side, be deaf to those calls.

They Died as Catholics.—" From amongst many

incidents that I could cite, let me take one. During the war of 1776 the king's house at Winchester was used as a prison for French prisoners of war. A dreadfully contagious fever broke out amongst them. Many of them died. They were chiefly Catholics, and were attended in their last moments by two or three Catholic priests residing in that city. But amongst the sick prisoners there were many Protestants; and these requested the attendance of Protestant parsons. There were the parsons of all the parishes at Winchester. There were the deans and all the prebendaries. But not a man of them went to console the dying Protestants, in consequence of which several of them desired the assistance of the priests and, of course, died Catholics. Dr. Milner, in his letter to Dr. Sturges (page 56), mentions this matter, and he says: 'The answer (of the Protestant parsons) I understand to have been this: "We are not more afraid, as individuals, to face death than the priests are: but we must not carry poisonous contagion into the bosoms of our families."' No, to be sure! But then, not to call this the cassock's taking shelter behind the petticoat, in what a dilemma does this place the Dean and Chapter! Either they neglected their most sacred duty, and left Protestants to flee, in their last moments, into the arms of 'Popery'; or, that clerical celibacy, against which they have declaimed all their lives, and still declaim, and still hold up to us, their flocks, as something both contemptible and wicked, is, after all, necessary to that 'care of souls,' to which they profess themselves to have been called, and for which they receive such munificent reward.

LITTLE OR NOTHING FOR THE POOR.—"But conclusive, perfectly satisfactory, as these reasons are, we should not, if we were to stop here, do anything like justice to our subject; for, as to the parochial clergy, do we not see, aye, and feel too, that they, if with families, or intending to have families, find little to spare to the poor of their flocks? In short, do we not know that a married priesthood and pauperism and poor rates, all came upon this country at one and the same moment? And what was the effect of clerical celibacy with regard to the higher orders of the clergy? A bishop, for instance, having neither wife nor child, naturally expended his resources amongst the people in his diocese. He spent a part of them on his Cathedral church, or in some other way sent his revenues back to the people. If William of Wyckham had been a married man, if the bishops in those days had been married men, the parsons would not now have had a college either at Eton, Westminster, Oxford, or Cambridge.

THE PROTESTANT BISHOP.—"Besides, who is to expect of human nature that a bishop with a wife and family will, in his distribution of Church preferment, consider nothing but the interest of religion? We are not to expect of man more than that of which we from experience know that man is capable. It is for the lawgiver to interpose, and to take care that the community suffer not from the frailty of the nature of individuals, whose private virtues even may, in some cases, and those not a few, not have a tendency to produce public good. I do not say that married bishops ever do wrong, because I am not acquainted with them well enough to ascertain the fact; but, in speaking of the diocese in which I was born, and in which I am best acquainted, I may say that it is certain that, if the late Bishop of Winchester had lived in Catholic times, he could not have had a wife, and that he could not have had a wife's sister, to marry Mr. Edmund Poulter, in which case I may be allowed to think it possible that Mr. Poulter would not have quitted the bar for the pulpit, and that he would not have had the two livings of Moon-Stoke and Soberton and a Prebend besides; that his son Brownlow Poulter would not have had the two livings of Buriton and Petersfield; that his son Charles Poulter would not have had the three livings of Alton, Binstead, and Kingsley; that his son-in-law Ogle would not have had the living of Bishop's Waltham! and that his son-in-law Haygarth would not have had the two livings of Upham and Durley.

BENEFICES KEPT IN THE FAMILY.—"That if the bishop had lived in Catholic times, he could not have had a son, Charles Augustus North, to have the two livings of Alverstoke and Havard, and to be a Prebend; that he could not have had another son, Francis North, to have the four livings of Old Alresford, Medstead, New Alresford, and St. Mary's, Southampton, and to be, moreover, a Prebend and Master of Saint Cross; that he could not have had a daughter to marry Mr. Wm. Garnier, to have the two livings of Droxford and Brightwell Baldwin, and to be a Prebend and a Chancellor besides; that he could not have had Mr. William Garnier's brother, Thomas Garnier, for a relation, and this latter might not then have had the two livings of Aldingbown and Bishop's Stoke; that he could not have another daughter to marry Mr. Thomas De Grey, to have the four livings of Calbourne, Fawley, Merton, and Rounton, and to be a Prebend and also an Archdeacon besides.

"In short, if the late Bishop had lived in Catholic times, it is a little too much to believe that these twenty-four livings, five Prebends, one Chancellorship, one Archdeaconship, and one Mastership, worth, perhaps, altogether, more than twenty thousand pounds a year, would have fallen to the ten persons above named. And may we not reasonably suppose that the bishop, instead of having behind him (as the newspapers told us he did) savings to nearly the amount of three hundred thousand pounds in money, would, if he had had no children nor grandchildren, have expended a part of this money on that ancient and magnificent Cathedral, the roof of which has recently been in danger of falling in, or would have been the founder of something for the public good and national honor, or would have been a most munificent friend and protector of the poor, and would never, at any rate, have suffered small beer to be sold out of his episcopal palace at Farnham! With an excise license, mind you!"

PLUNDERING THE MONASTERIES.—Mr. Cobbett shows how the "Reformation" in England had suppressed the monastic institutions and robbed the poor of the sustenance they drew from the monasteries. He shows, too, how far removed from saints were the Protestant soldiers who carried out the desecration.

"Never, in all probability," he continues at page 85, "since the world began, was there so rich a harvest of plunder. The ruffians of Cromwell entered the convent, they tore down the altars to get away the gold and silver; ransacked the chests and drawers of the monks and nuns; tore off the covers of books that were ornamented with precious metals. . . The ready money, in the convents, down to the last shilling, was seized. In short, the most rapacious and unfeeling soldiery never, in towns delivered up to be sacked, proceeded with greediness, shamelessness, and brutality to be at all compared with those of these heroes of the Protestant Reformation ; and this, observe, towards persons, women as well as men, who had committed no crime known to the laws, who had no crime regularly laid to their charge, who had had no hearing in their defence, a large part of whom had, within a year, been declared, by this same parliament, to lead most godly and useful lives, the whole of whose possessions were guaranteed to them by the Great Charter, as much as the King's crown was to him, and whose estates were enjoyed for the benefit of the poor, as well as for that of these plundered possessors themselves.

" . . . . . . of all the scourges that ever afflicted this country, [England] none is to be put in comparison with the Protestant 'Reformation.'

" . . . the thing impudently called the 'Reformation.'"

THE HORRIBLE DOCTRINE OF MALTHUS.—After this Mr. Cobbett alludes to the doctrine of Malthus for the suppression of children, which numbers of English Protestants approved of. He says at page 61:—

"Enough now, about the celibacy of the clergy, but it is impossible to quit the subject without one word to Parson Malthus. . . Now, he wants to compel the laboring classes to refrain to a great extent from marriage; and Mr. Scarlett actually brought a Bill into parliament, having, in one part of it, this avowed object in view; the great end, proposed by both, being to cause a diminution of the poor rates. Parson Malthus does not call this recommending celibacy; but 'moral restraint.' And, what is celibacy but moral restraint! So that here are these people reviling the Catholic Church for insisting on vows of celibacy on the part of those who choose to be priests, or nuns; and, at the same time, proposing to compel the laboring classes to live in a state of celibacy, or to run the manifest risk of perishing, they and their children, from starvation!

"Is all this sheer impudence, or is it sheer folly? One or the other; it is greater than ever was before heard from the lips of mortal man. They affect to believe that the clerical vow of celibacy must be nugatory, because nature is constantly at work to overcome it. This is what Dr. Sturges asserts. Now, if this be the case with men of education, men on whom their religion imposes abstinence, fasting, almost constant prayer, and an exceeding number of austerities; if this be the case with regard to such men, and if it be, therefore, contemptible and wicked, not to compel them, mind, to make such vows, but to permit them voluntarily to do it, what must it be to compel young men and women laborers to live in a state of celibacy, or be exposed to absolute starvation? Why, the answer is, that it is the grossest inconsistency, or premeditated wickedness; but that, like all the other wild schemes and crude projects relative to the poor, we trace it at once back to the 'Reformation,' that great source of the poverty, and misery, and degradation of the main body of the people of this kingdom. . . . .

PROLIFIC IN MISFORTUNE.—" But of all its consequences that of introducing a married clergy has, perhaps, been the most prolific of mischief. This has absolutely erected an order for the procreation of dependents on the state; for the procreation of thousands of persons annually, who have no fortunes of their own, and who must be, somehow or other, maintained by burdens imposed upon the people. . . . .

". . . and, after all that we have, during our whole lives, heard against that rule (celibacy) of the Catholic Church, which imposed a vow of celibacy on those who choose the clerical or the monastic life, we find, whether we look at this rule in a religious, in a moral, in a civil, or in a political point of view, that it was founded in wisdom, that it was a great blessing to the people at large, and that its abolition is a thing to be deeply deplored."

No Influence with the Masses.—And now let us put this question:—Has the Protestant Church, the majority of whose members are so bitter against the confessional, and who so strongly condemn clerical celibacy, become popular with the masses, and is it strong in beneficent influences? Let a Protestant answer the query.

The Rev. Dr. John H. Oerter has recently written a book on "The Social Question in the Light of History and the Word of Truth." He says of his Church:—

"That under the present emergency a solemn obligation rests with the Church of the Lord Jesus Christ, only ignorance and selfishness can deny. But in speaking of the Church we refer principally to the Evangelical portion thereof. For it is a well-known fact that the Catholic Church long ago has initiated measures to counteract the subversive influences of the present social commotions, and, if possible, to turn them to her own advantage. And what is still more important, we have to face the humiliating truth that the ranks of socialism and anarchism are mostly swelled by former members of the Protestant persuasion. This sad fact ought to induce the Evangelical Church above all others to awaken to a sense of her duty and to strain every nerve to counter-influence the growing evil. But in order to be fitted for such an important work it is absolutely necessary that the evil should be discerned and traced to its proper source."

The Power of Example.—We have shown in these

pages the power of example, the great good that a devoted clergy, continent and self-sacrificing, can achieve to make men and women better, to induce them to resist the ordinary temptations of the flesh as well as the extraordinary and peculiar temptations to follow the false philosophy of modern times. Dr. Oerter goes on :—

"The sad position of the laborer in the present commotion, especially the fact that the *great mass of the poor working class have become estranged from the* [Protestant] *Church*, ought to cause her to seriously reflect whether she has always made that dependent class of society the special object of tender care and watchfulness, which, according to the illustrious example of the great Head of the Church and the explicit command of the word of life, it is entitled to."

Dr. Oerter struggles hard to combat a popular theory, as may be seen from the following passage :—

"The laboring class must be convinced that it is an utterly unfounded and malicious charge on the part of some demagogic leaders that Christianity was exclusively a religion for the rich, and that the clergy and the Church—the Church of the lowly and hardworking Jesus of Nazareth—stood with their sympathies on the side of cold-hearted capitalism.

"The glaring inconsistency of many a so-called Church member has increased the bitterness of the masses against the Word of Life and robbed them of the last remnant of confidence in the [Protestant] Church and her saving work."

Dr. Oerter says that deeds and not words are necessary to bring back the strayed sheep. Well, the Catholic Church is doing her share, and the celibacy of her clergy is one of the greatest instruments she possesses for preaching virtue by example.

# CHAPTER XII.

## Marriage and Divorce.

LAWS OF THE CHURCH AND STATE—MARRIAGE HONORED AND REVERED BY CATHOLICS, LIGHTLY REGARDED BY OTHERS—CHRIST FORBIDS DIVORCE—ADVICE OF THE CHURCH TO THOSE ABOUT-TO MARRY.

Origen regarded celibacy as rather springing from a desire to serve God without the interruptions arising from the cares of marriage than from asceticism, and promptly condemned those who abandoned their wives, even from the highest motives. The Church has always encouraged marriage among the laity, and her wisest teachers have ever reproved those who, through mistaken zeal, have enjoined the opposite or extreme asceticism. For instance, Dionysius of Corinth was obliged to reprove Pinytus, Bishop of Gnosus, for endeavoring to render celibacy obligatory upon his people, to the manifest danger of those whose virtue was less austere.

MARRIAGE A SACRAMENT.—It does not follow, as many thoughtless opponents would have it follow, that, because the Catholic Church imposes celibacy on her priests, therefore she is careless about or indifferent to marriage as regards others. On the contrary, obeying the law of her Divine Founder, she has made marriage a sacrament, whereas, in other Churches, it is looked upon as little better than a civil contract. St. Paul said: "This is a great sacrament."—Ephes. v.

Again she is the only church which does not recognize divorce. She has taken literally the words of our Lord:—"Whom God has joined together let no man put asunder." She holds that death alone can put an end to marriage. One of the most distinguished ornaments the French pulpit has had was Père Bourdaloue, of the Society of Jesus. In discussing the sacrament of matrimony he used to beg his hearers to consider seriously what such an engagement was, what such a servitude was for all one's life, without redress.

"There is no vow," he said, "how solemn soever, with which the Church may not dispense; but as to marriage, her hands are, as I may say, tied, her power not extending so far. It was an engagement which appeared to the Apostles of such consequence that they judged the state of celibacy preferable to it. 'If the case of the man be so with his wife, it is not good to marry.'—Matt. xix. And what reply did our Saviour make? Did he blame this sentiment, so unfavorable to matrimony? He approved of it; he confirmed it; he congratulated them upon their having comprehended what others were unable to comprehend:—'All men cannot take this saying.'—Matt. xix. The reason of it is, that they plainly saw how heavy a burden it would prove for the greater part of those who should receive this sacrament."

ITS TREMENDOUS RESPONSIBILITIES.—But for those who are able to enter into matrimony, for those who are entitled to do so, the Church has sanctified that state. Her priests, her bishops, and her Popes have explained its tremendous responsibilities, and have laid down the rules by which they may be successfully borne. St.

Augustine wrote a tract on the nuptial state. "A threefold good," he said, "accrues from matrimony—posterity, fidelity, a sacrament. And, indeed, it is a great happiness for mankind that Almighty God, by the institution of a sacrament, has established connections and alliances among them; and that he has raised these connections and alliances to a supernatural order, by a grace which enables them to obtain these blessings. Besides which it is an advantage greatly deserving of esteem for persons engaged in the matrimonial state to think that another person upon earth has plighted them their troth, and, though nothing to them in the order of nature or by proximity of blood, yet owes them everything, love, respect, mutual assistance, fidelity. Finally, I hold that God does honor to fathers and mothers by choosing them to bring up in the marriage state a lawful progeny, that is, servants by whom he is glorified and His Church augmented."

A SPECIAL GRACE SANCTIFIES IT.—Rev. Dr. Alzog, whom we have quoted elsewhere, says in his "Universal Church History" (Vol. 1. p. 450):—"The Catholic Church, instinctively faithful to the doctrine of Christ and the teaching of His Apostles, has indeed always regarded virginity as a supernatural gift and prerogative, and in pagan times appealed to its practice in evidence of the divine and subduing influence of the Gospel; but in all this it has never been her purpose to detract from the dignity and sanctity of matrimony. Quite the contrary, for she teaches that a special grace of the Holy Ghost sanctifies the union of man and wife. * * * St. Ignatius taught that it should be contracted in presence of a bishop, and Tertullian and Clement of Alexandria speak distinctly and particularly of the bishop's blessing it. Marriage, contracted with these precautions and observances, was regarded as valid, pleasing in the sight of Heaven, and indissoluble even after conjugal fidelity had been outraged. It is plainly affirmed in the Pastor of Hermas, and by Clement of Alexandria, that if, after a divorce, any of the parties should contract a new marriage during the lifetime of the other, such marriage is, according to the passage in Matt. v. 32, an adultery."

The doctrine of the indissolubility of marriage was the abiding belief and sentiment of the early Christians. As time went on, some Churches began to entertain a doubt on this point. The Eastern Church put an interpretation upon the passages in Matt. v. 32,—"But I say unto you that whosoever shall put away his wife, saving for the cause of fornication, causeth her to commit adultery, and whosoever shall marry her that is divorced, committeth adultery," and Matt. xix. 7,—"They say unto him, why did Moses then command to give a writing of divorcement, and to put her away," favorable to divorce, which was sanctioned by imperial law. But the Western Church of Rome and Africa clung to the Apostolic and Evangelic tradition, insisting upon the absolute and unconditional indissolubility of marriage, and punished with excommunication those who attempted any violation of this fundamental law. Dr. Alzog says this is clear from the declarations of the Popes Innocent and Leo, and from the canon of the Synod of Mileve (A. D. 416).

PROHIBITED MARRIAGES.—Although the early Fathers of the Church prohibited marriages between Christians and either pagans or Jews, and also heretics, yet the prohibition was only disciplinary and did not invalidate the marriage contract. In Gaul and Spain, during the sixth and seventh centuries, marriages between Catholics and either pagans or Jews were forbidden under penalty of excommunication, and the penalty was not removed until a separation had taken place. The Synods of Elvira, Chalcedon, and Agde also prohibited marriages between Catholics and heretics, but these were never regarded as invalid.

VALIDITY AND CONTRACT.—The conditions of the validity of marriage are mostly identical with the conditions which determine the validity of contracts in general. The consent to the union must be mutual, voluntary, deliberate, and manifested by external signs. The signs of consent need not be verbal in order to make the marriage valid, though the rubric of the Ritual requires the consent to be expressed in that manner. The consent must be to actual marriage then and there, not at some future time; for in the latter case we should have engagement to marry, or betrothal, not marriage itself. Consent to marry, if a certain condition in the past or present be realized, (*e. g.*, " I take N. for my wife, if you are the daughter of M. and N.") suffices, supposing that the condition be fulfilled. Nay, it is generally held that, if a condition be added dependent on future contingencies, (*e. g.*, " I take you N. for my wife, if your father will give you such and such a dowry,") the marriage becomes a reality. The condition appended, however, must not be contrary to the essence of marriage, *e. g.*, a man cannot take a woman for his wife, to have and hold just as long as he pleases. (See Gury, "Theol. Moral.", De Matrimon., cap. iii.).

When Our Lord condemns the Pharisaic immorality, annuls the Mosaic dispensation, and declares, " Whosoever shall put away his wife, except for fornication, and shall marry another, committeth adultery, and he who marrieth her when she is put away committeth adultery," the Catholic understands him to mean that the bond of marriage is always, even when one of the wedded parties has proved unfaithful, indissoluble. From the first, Christ's declaration made the practice of Christians with regard to divorce essentially and conspicuously different from those of their heathen and Jewish neighbors. Still it was only by degrees that the strict practices or even the strict theory just stated were accepted in the Church. And before we enter on the interpretation of Christ's words, we will give a sketch of the history of practice and opinion on the matter.

REGULATING DIVORCE.—Christian princes had, of course, to deal with the subject of divorce, but they did not at once recast the old laws on Christian principles. Constantine, Theodosius the Younger, and Valentinian III. forbade divorce except on certain specified grounds; other emperors, like Anastasius (in 497) and Justin (whose law was in force till 900) permitted divorce by mutual consent, but no one emperor limited divorce to the single case of adultery. Chardon says that divorce (of course *a vincula*) was allowed among the Ostrogoths in Spain till the thirteenth century, in France under the first and second dynasties, in Germany till the seventh century, in Britain till the tenth. (Chardon, "Hist. des Sacraments," tom. v., Marriage, ch. 5.) It would be a waste of labor to accumulate quotations from the Fathers in proof of their belief that divorce was unlawful except in the case of adultery. But it is very important to notice that the oldest traditions, both of the Greek and Latin Churches, regarded marriage as absolutely indissoluble. Thus the "Pastor Hermæ" (lib. ii., Mand. iv., c. 1,) Athanagoras, "Legat." 33, (whose testimony, however, does not count for much, since he objected to second marriages altogether,) and Tertullian ("De Monog." 9,) who speaks in this place, as the context shows, for the Catholic Church, teach this clearly and unequivocally. The principle is recognized in the Apostolic Canons (Canon 48, al. 47,) by the Council of Elvira, held at the beginning of the fourth century, Canon 9 (which, however, only speaks of a woman who has left an unfaithful husband), and by other early authorities.

ADULTERY AND SECOND MARRIAGE.—However, the Eastern Christians, though not in the earliest times, came to understand our Lord's words as permitting a second marriage in the case of adultery, which was supposed to dissolve the marriage bond altogether. Such is the view and practice of the Greek and Oriental sects at the present day. And even in certain parts of the West similar views prevailed for a time. Many French synods (*e. g.*, those of Vannes in 465, and of Compiègne, in 756) allow the husband of a wife who has been unfaithful to marry again in her life-time. Nay, the latter council permitted remarriage in other cases:—if a woman had a husband struck by leprosy and got leave from him to marry another, or if a man had given his wife leave to go into in a convent (Canons 16 and 19).

Pope Gregory II., in a letter to St. Boniface, in the year 726, recommended that the husband of a wife seized by sickness which prevented cohabitation should not marry again, but left him free to do so, provided he maintained his first wife. (Quoted by Hefele, "Beiträge," vol. ii., p. 376). At Florence the question of divorce was discussed between the Latins and Greeks, but after the decree of Union, and it is not known what answers the Greeks gave on the matter.

The Council of Trent confirmed the present doctrine and discipline, which had long prevailed in the West, in the following words: " If any man say that the Church is in error because it has taught and teaches, following the doctrine of the Gospels and the Apostles, that the bond of marriage cannot be dissolved because of the adultery of one or both parties, let him be anathema." (Sess. xxiv., De Matrim. can. 5). The studious moderation of language here is obvious, for the canon does not directly require any doctrine to be accepted; it only anathematizes those who condemn a certain doctrine, and implies that this doctrine is taught by the Church and derived from Christ. It was the Venetian ambassadors who prevailed on the Fathers to draw up the canon in this indirect form, so as to avoid needless offence to the Greek subjects of Venice, in Cyprus, Candia, Corfu, Zante, and Cephalonia. The canon was no doubt chiefly meant to stem the erroneous views on divorce of Lutherans and Calvinists.

THE ROMAN LAWS.—The effect of the spread of Christianity was to re-invest marriage with the religious character from which in the later law of Rome it had completely escaped. The history of divorce in modern times has been the gradual decay outside the Catholic Church of the restrictions which were thought appropriate to the religious character of the institution of marriage. In Roman law marriage was regarded as a voluntary union, which might be terminated at any time by the consent of the parties. No legal process was required, although the abuse of the power of divorce was sometimes punished. Justinian settled the grounds of divorce as follows :—

The wife could divorce her husband—(1), for conspiracy against the empire; (2), attempting her life; (3), attempting to induce her to commit adultery; (4), wrongfully accusing her of adultery; (5), taking a paramour to his house, or frequenting any other house in the same town with a paramour. On a divorce for these reasons the wife recovered her dowry, and obtained the husband's portion as well. If she was divorced for other reasons she forfeited her dowry, and could not marry for five years, as in the legislation of Theodosius and Valentinian. So a husband might justly divorce his wife for—(1), concealment of plots against the empire; (2), adultery; (3), attempting her husband's life, or concealing plots against him; (4), going to baths or banquets with other men; (5), remaining from home against her husband's wish; (6), going to circus, theatre, or amphitheatre against his wish.

A very interesting commentary on contemporary manners are the reasons given above for divorce. These experiments in divorce legislation display anxiety to regulate the relationship of marriage as a purely civil institution, with a view mainly to public decorum and the comfort of individuals.

THE CHANGE OF THE CANON LAW.—But great was the change from the pure Roman law to the canon law. The ceremony became sacred, the tie indissoluble. Those whom God hath joined let no man put assunder, was the first text of the new law of marriage, and against such a prohibition social convenience and experience pleaded in vain, so far as the Catholic Church was concerned. It is different in other Churches. Says a Protestant writer, Professor Edward Robertson: "In countries which have embraced the doctrines of the Reformation, a relaxation of the law of divorce has generally followed the change of religion—whether immediately, as in Scotland, or indirectly, as in England. In Roman Catholic countries the theory of the canon law still rules."

But in Protestant England the change of religion bore

heavily in this as in other things on the poor. It was only the rich who could obtain divorce. The poor were driven to bigamy, says the writer just quoted. Divorce was an expensive luxury, and a great number of forms had to be observed to obtain it.

A SATIRE ON THE ENGLISH LAW.—The satirical address of Mr. Justice Maule to a poor man convicted of bigamy, in 1845, put the absurdities of the existing English law in a very glaring light. The prisoner's wife had robbed him and had run away with another man. "You should have brought an action," said the Justice, "and obtained damages, which the other side would probably not have been able to pay, and you would have had to pay your own costs, perhaps £100 or £150. You should then have gone to the ecclesiastical courts and obtained a divorce *a mensa et thoro*, and then to the House of Lords, where, having proved that these preliminaries had been complied with, you would have been enabled to marry again. The expense might have amounted to £500 or £600, or perhaps £1,000. You say you are a poor man. But I must tell you that there is not one law for the rich and another for the poor."

PREVALENCE OF DIVORCE AMONG PROTESTANTS.— It was not until 1857, that an Act of Parliament established the Divorce Court, and now divorces in England are as plentiful as blackberries. Divorce in Scotland had the effect of remitting the parties to the state of unmarried persons. The law, however, made one exception. A divorced person was not allowed to marry the paramour, at all events if the paramour was named in the decree, and for this reason the name of the paramour is sometimes omitted, so that the parties may be allowed to marry if they wish.

In this country the law of divorce varies in different

states. Each state determines for itself the causes for which divorce may be granted. In most states it appears to be allowed not only for adultery, but for cruelty, wilful desertion, habitual drunkenness, neglect, refusal, or inability to maintain one's wife. Perhaps there is no other country in which divorce is so easily obtained as in America. The "Divorce Mill" of Chicago is a standing reproach to us.

In France divorce was allowed after the Revolution, but soon the old canon law was re-inforced and still prevails.

DR. TALMAGE ON MARRIAGE.—The number of ruined homes in America because of the lightness and indifference with which marriage is regarded and the great facilities for divorce have often been commented upon. Let us take the testimony of a popular Protestant minister, who has been heard on both sides of the Atlantic. The Rev. Dr. De Witt Talmage, of Brooklyn, preaching in the beginning of the present year (1888) said :—

"Theologians have differed upon and discussed this subject and offered various explanations, but I will not be drawn into the discussion, I will not be diverted from the tremendous fact, about which there is no dispute, that it is a terrible, a fearful thing to vow a vow."

Speaking of the terrible consequences of broken vows he said that the wards of our asylums were filled with unfortunate females who were the victims of broken vows. This minister fully recognized the looseness of the marriage tie in his own Church. "There are parts of this country where promise of marriage," said the preacher, "is treated very much as a joke. The joke has, unhappily, too often disastrous consequences.

I hold that in nine hundred and ninty-nine cases out of a thousand promise to marry is as sacred and as binding as marriage itself. You do not treat lightly your promise in business matters. You do not neglect your promissory note. Your house might be lost if you did. Will you compare the heart and the happiness of a man or woman with a house? The most shameful, the most disgraceful of all lies is a broken espousal. But, you say, 'suppose I change my mind on reconsidering matters.' I care not for what reason you change your mind. You made the vow, and you will be held responsible if you live, or whether you live or not."

The Doctor told a story of a man who broke his first vow, and who, making and carrying out a second engagement, spent his life in repeating the experience of Shakespeare's "Taming of the Shrew." "Make no rash vows," said the Doctor, "but when you make a promise keep it. I will not say that there are not exceptional cases. But I will say that in the great majority of cases broken vows must be followed by punishment."

"The great trouble," continues the preacher, "is that there is too much frivolity about this matter. It is a kind of frivolity that too often results in a kind of hell upon earth, where the devil has things all his own way. It is high time that the pulpit should make itself heard in tones of thunder. Public sentiment is loose on the subject, and I denounce the sentiment that prevails.

LOOK BEFORE YOU LEAP.—"Some of you are saying: 'Suppose we find out something wrong after we have vowed the vow. Is it not wiser to break the vow in time than to enter upon an arrangement from which nothing but misery can result?' Nonsense!

Find out in time. You have abundance of opportunity. If you cannot find out in time and before you make the vow you are much better fitted for a lunatic asylum than for marriage. Don't marry till you get an undisputed title."

The preacher called especially upon women to beware. Men could get away sometimes from the unpleasantness. They could go to the club. They could smoke themselves stupid, they could drink themselves drunk. But women had to stay and endure. Carpet knights, he said, were to be avoided by the one sex, and that most God-forsaken of all women, the flirt, was to be avoided by the other sex.

A DANGEROUS STATE.—According to the opinion of the Fathers and of Christian moralists, if every state be exposed to danger, then matrimony is one of the most dangerous. The point is to reconcile conjugal liberty with continence and chastity; a true and intimate friendship for a creature with an inviolable fidelity to the Creator; an exact, diligent, watchful care of temporal affairs with an external disengagement from the things of this world.

INCONTINENCE OF MATRIMONY—"The first danger," says Bourdaloue, "is the incontinence of matrimony. St. Jerome, writing to a virgin, and instructing her in the duties of celibacy, a state in which she professed to live, was not afraid to express his thoughts in certain terms that might hurt her delicacy. And he gave for reason that he deemed it better to run the hazard of not speaking with sufficient reserve, than to hide truths from her which immediately concerned her eternal welfare. And, perhaps, he had good reason to deliver himself of that letter. * * * Matrimony is a state of chastity and continence, as well as celibacy, whatever difference there may be between them in other respects. There are laws in matrimony ordained by God which it is not allowable to trangress. All the irregularities committed in matrimony, far from being excused, or in some shape justified by the sacrament, contract thereby a particular malignity and deformity."

CONJUGAL CHASTITY.—Let us ask our readers if any minister of God is justified in voluntarily running the risk of adding to the occasions of sin? Here are matrimonial laws, which, as Bourdaloue observes, it is a grievous sin to break. The priest, by marrying, runs into temptation. In the unmarried state he is free from such temptation. As an an athlete strengthens his body by constant exercise, so the soul of the unmarried priest is strengthened by continual continence. This particular occasion of sin is always absent; therefore, the easier it is for him to serve God with a pure heart and to edify others by his example. St. Jerome says of the three kinds of chastity—virginity, widowhood, and matrimony—conjugal chastity, though the most imperfect, is yet the most difficult; because, he adds, it is much easier to abstain entirely than behave moderately and renounce absolutely the flesh, the domestic enemy, than prescribe its laws and repress its sallies. Virginity, says St. Jerome, by preserving itself, subdues almost without fighting. Hardly is it acquainted with the danger, because it keeps at a remote distance. The same may be said proportionately of widowhood. But the case is entirely different with respect to conjugal chastity. "Between that and impurity there is only a step," is the commentary of Bardaloue, "but a step that leads to a crime deserving of eternal woe."

All who enter the clerical state are not perfect. Some

ministers and some priests cannot wholly repress their passions and animosities. Left to themselves and making a sincere effort they may succeed. With a companion, like a wife, who feels bound to flatter them, or at least to fall into their whims, their passions are more or less inflamed, their sinful inclinations more or less helped along. The union brings sin to another. The Catholic celibate, if he sins at all, sins alone. The married minister causes another to share in his sinful thoughts and acts. Nay, should his children be old enough to share in his animosities and passions he brings sin to several. Can you not see, therefore, how great is the danger that lurks in matrimony for the priest?

MUTUAL FELLOWSHIP.—To this first danger, incontinence, which Bourdaloue has referred to, he adds another which is in the same train of thought we have expressed. "It is," says the great French pulpiteer, "mutual fellowship, of which the effect should be so perfect a union of hearts, that for your spouse you should be disposed to give up everything, to sacrifice everything, but with this exception, so rare and delicate, that conjugal love does not supersede the love of God; that man and wife should be so affected one to another that at the same time both one and the other be still more strongly affected to God; that a wife disposed to follow all the reasonable inclinations of her husband, have still fortitude enough to resist him whenever he would have her fall in with his passions, bear a part in his irregularities, lend an ear to his defamatory or impious discourses, join in his resentments, or be aiding his revenge. Accordingly, when your husband has received an injury, when he has been unjustly offended or outraged, it is allowable for you to be affected with his case, to partake in his afflictions, to procure him just and suitable satisfaction; this you may do; nay, this you are bound to do. But to proceed farther: to adopt his animosities and aversions, to abet his frantic sallies and violence, to agree to everything which an embittered and inflamed heart inspires, is not to behave like a Christian woman."

The celibate priest, when his passions are touched, can retire to solitude to pray and to wrestle with his feelings. The chances are that he will conquer. The married minister sits down with his wife, and naturally pours into her ear what has affected him, and the chances are that her affection for him may rouse in her resentment against those who have offended him. And so there is a double sin. But even should he retire to his "study" (what a miserable substitute for the sanctuary of the altar!) to pray, his meditations may be interrupted by his children, and so the occasion lost for the strengthening of good resolves.

PLEASING ONLY HER HUSBAND.—And this is what St. Paul meant to teach the Corinthians when he made the happiness of virgins to consist in not being divided between God and the world, and in not being charged with the obligation and care of pleasing men, but only Jesus Christ, the spouse of their souls:—"And the unmarried woman and the virgin thinketh on the things of the Lord."—(I. Cor. vii.) St. Paul points out that a married woman is always at a loss how to preserve, at the same time, the affection of her husband and the favor of God; being obliged to preserve, so far as she is able, both the one and the other, and yet not knowing, on a thousand occasions, how to reconcile both obligations. She may give up God to please her husband. Then, should she have strength to resist her husband, dissensions arise, and sin is added to sin.

Some years ago two continents rang with a great Protestant scandal. Far be it from us to say one word against the late Rev. Henry Ward Beecher. He was a great preacher, and a man of great charity. But what we wish to emphasize is this: that, because he was a married minister, the charge against him in reference to Mrs. Tilton was made all the more of. Had he been an unmarried minister the case would not have received the great prominence it did. No Catholic priest of the same degree of popularity had ever been placed in so embarrassing a position.

PROVIDING FOR HIS OFFSPRING.—The idea of the world, and to a large extent it is a just one, is that a husband should give up everything for his wife. Of course, this does not include honor and virtue, but what is understood is that a husband should devote himself so completely to the happiness of his wife and family, that he has no care or thought for anything, save in so far as it promotes the object of his life. It is the duty of a father of a family to attend strictly to his business, so that there may be an adequate provision for his wife (should he die first) and for his offspring. A married clergyman who does his whole duty in this respect to his family, who is compelled to engage in some professional pursuit to supplement a possibly small salary, cannot do his whole duty to his God and the souls committed to his care. If, on the other hand, he devotes himself exclusively to religion, the interests of his family must suffer. What right, then, has he to marry, to bring children into the world, knowing at the outset, from the nature of his calling, that he cannot have the time or the opportunity to provide for a family? It is a divided allegiance, and, if his soul be a sensitive one, must bring him only grief in the end.

EDUCATION OF CHILDREN.—The education of children lays a strict obligation on the father of attending to temporal affairs. The obligation is a rock against which it is no easy matter to avoid splitting. "Who cannot see," says Père Bourdaloue, "the extreme difficulty of reconciling together the care of property and a disengagement from that same property? According to the gospel, if you neglect to provide for your children in a manner suitable to their condition, you incur guilt in the presence of God; and if again, with the view of providing for your children, you suffer your heart to be possessed with a desire of the love of riches, you have no right to or hope of salvation. In the marriage state you are not allowed, as others are, to relinquish everything in order to follow Jesus Christ. You must possess, you must preserve, you must labor in a reasonable manner to acquire; but in possessing, preserving and acquiring, you must wean your heart from all terrene affections. So speaks St. Paul. Hearken to his words:—

"'This, therefore, I say brethren, it remaineth that those who have wives be as though they had none; and they who buy, as though they possessed not; and they who use this world, as though they used it not.'—I. Cor. vii.

"The reason of it is given by the same Apostle:—

"'For the figure of this world passeth away.'—I. Cor. vii.

"And for my part I am bold enough to add, applying to you this point of doctrine, that the attention which you may give, and which you ought to give, to the things of this world, takes off in no manner the obligation of renouncing them in heart and will. This our Blessed Saviour made a general law for all mankind; and as this law, St. Chrysostom tells us, cannot mean a real and effective renunciation, it must be understood necessarily of mental renunciation: 'He that forsaketh not all.'"—Luke xiv.

A CUMBROUS DUTY.—Truly, the bringing up of children, whether regular or irregular in their conduct and behavior, is generally for parents a cumbrous duty and a heavy cross. "What a melancholy thing it is," says Bourdaloue, "to have a numerous family, and to want the means of providing for them! To have children capable of any business and not be able to procure them employment! To be under the necessity of letting them pass their days in a constrained idleness and obscurity, in which their birth, the credit of their family, and their personal merit are buried and lost! What sorrow and regret, when an unforeseen accident, an unexpected death, snatches away children all at once, on whom their parents doted and built their fondest hopes!"

How can a married minister do his duty to his parishioners under these circumstances? Must he not and will he not devote most of his attention to keeping away and preserving his children from whatever may corrupt their hearts—domestic irregularities, loose conversation, dangerous company, obscene plays, bad books? Naturally his heart will be more with them than with his flock.

UNSYMPATHETIC HEARTS.—We have already said that the young clergyman in his choice of a companion is guided more by impulse than reason. Few men will marry an ugly woman simply because of her qualities of head and heart. Dwelling upon this companionship, Bourdaloue observes:—"If we find it difficult to bear with ourselves, shall we find it easier to bear with another? Of so many marriages which we see contracted every day, how many are cemented by a sympathy of hearts? And should there be an antipathy, what martyrdom can be more cruel. This is the most deplorable circumstance of all, that these domestic trials and contradictions but serve to keep you farther away from God, and to make you the more criminal in his divine presence. Thus circumstanced, married persons seek comfort abroad; they turn their inclinations into another channel, and what irregularities does not this draw after it! What animosities and aversions do they not harbor in their breasts! With what murmurs and complaints, in what distress, despair, and resentment, is a long succession of years run out! They remain in these dispositions till death; and (as St. Bernard said) all they do is to go from one hell to another, from a hell of sin and wickedness to a hell of pains and punishments, from the hell of matrimony to the hell of the devils and the damned."

THERE IS NO PROTESTANT BOURDALOUE.—Who will regard matrimony lightly and say it is good for all conditions of men and women after studying these words of Bourdaloue? And who was this great French preacher. Not a clergyman with a taint upon his character, not a fanatic, not an ignorant man, not a priest under censure. He was one of the most illustrious men of his time. At the age of sixteen, he entered the Society of Jesus and there completed his studies. His able masters, who early discerned his talents, successively confided to him the chairs of humanity, rhetoric, philosophy, and moral theology. Bourdaloue suddenly appeared in the midst of the glories and fascinations of the court of Louis XIV., but never failed in denouncing the follies and vices of the age. After the revocation of the Edict of Nantes, he was sent to Languedoc to preach to the Protestants and confirm the newly converted in the Catholic faith. " And in this delicate mission," says a Protestant writer, "he managed to reconcile the interests of his ministry with the sacred rights of humanity." In the later years of his life he abandoned the pulpit and devoted himself to charitable assemblies, hospitals, and prisons. Can our adversaries point to such a man on their side, who has been praised by Lord Brougham, and whom later critics have held up as a model of virtue, eloquence, and learning?

Could Bourdaloue have been as great had he been a married man? Could he have cultivated his gifts had he mingled with the world? Cicero supplies the answer in a passage preserved by St. Augustine:— "Corporeal pleasures," says the eloquent Roman, "are incompatible with great thought. For how can a man give himself up to these kind of pleasures, and at the same time exercise his brain in thinking and reasoning?"

CELIBACY AND GENIUS.—"He who abandons himself to the pleasures of the flesh," says St. Chrysostom, "and who fixes his mind upon worldly objects, can conceive nothing that is great and exalted." "The *savant*," says St. Jerome, "ought not to marry, otherwise, no more philosophical studies for him. It is impossible for him to give himself up at the same time to his books and his wife."

In modern times men of letters abstain from marriage, lest it should interfere with their studies. With little money, they feel that the cares of a family, added to their own, would change that independent feeling without which their talent could not be exercised, and their genius have full scope. Without this clerical celibacy, should we have had those magnificent libraries that adorn our great cities, those grand products of the Christian mind. And those immortal works of antiquity, would they not have perished were it not for the monasteries? The revival of literature in France, which is a part of France's glory, was due entirely to the clergy. Should we have had so many daring missionaries, opening up new countries to our view, if marriage instead of celibacy had been the rule? Should we have had self-sacrificing priests going beyond the seas, penetrating savage regions, exposing themselves to all kinds of sufferings, to tortures, and death, and all for the glory of God, if they had had wives and children. Should we have had an Augustine in England, a Boniface in Germany, a Denis in France, if they had had families?

It is not necessary to state the conclusion—it is self-evident.

AN AID TO GOVERNMENT.—The priesthood is a necessity in the government of man, and the priesthood, if not continent, is absolutely worthless. Says the Count de Maistre, and the statement is worth considering :—

"What is the religious state in Catholic countries? So to speak an ennobled serfdom. To the ancient institution itself, so useful in many respects, this state adds a number of particular advantages, and removes it from all abuses. The vow of religion, instead of degrading man, sanctifies him. Instead of enslaving him to the vices of others, it emancipates him from them. In subjecting him to an elected superior, it declares him free in regard to other men, with whom he can no longer have any transaction. As often as the wills of men can be subdued without degrading the individual an inestimable service is rendered to society in relieving the government of the care of watching over these men, of employing, and especially of paying them. Never was there a happier idea than that of uniting in one body a number of peaceful citizens who labor, pray, study, write, give alms, cultivate the ground, and ask nothing of authority.

OVERCROWDED PROFESSIONS.—" This truth is particularly apparent in our days, when from all quarters men are throwing themselves upon the resources of the government, which knows not how to dispose of them. Our youth, impetuous, innumerable, unfortunately for itself, crowd into the career of public employments. There are four or five times more candidates than is necessary for every imaginable profession. You will not find an office in Europe [and the French author could add in America] in which the number of persons employed has not tripled or quadrupled within fifty years. Public business, it is said, has increased; but men create all this business, and too many interfere in it. All, at the same time, hasten towards power and the duties therewith connected: they forcibly open every door and necessitate the creation of new places; there is too much liberty, too much movement, too many wills let loose in the world. A mob of fools have inquired 'of what use are religious people?' How then! may not men serve the Church without being invested with a charge? And is the chaining up the passions and neutralizing vice of no consideration? Hundreds and hundreds of writers have pointed out, in the clearest manner, the numerous services the religious state has rendered to society; but I think it advantageous to make it be considered in the view that has been hitherto least attended to, and which, assuredly, was not the least important—as master and director of a multitude of wills—as an invaluable supplement to government, whose greatest interest it is to moderate the internal movement of the state, and to increase the number of men who have nothing to ask of it."—(The Pope.)

# CHAPTER XIII.

## Sensational Slanders.

THE LATEST AND WORST ATTACKS ON CATHOLIC PRACTICES—RIDICULOUS ALLEGATIONS ABOUT THE CONFESSIONAL AND SEMINARIES—A BRILLIANT LIST OF CONVERTS TO CATHOLICITY REFUTES THE FALSE CHARGES—IGNORANCE AND MENDACITY.

"Protestants and the followers of the Voltairian philosophy," says the Abbé Jager, "have not understood the reasons for celibacy. Most of them have looked upon it simply as a political movement on the part of Rome. Often our theologians, in arguing with them, have advanced against them only the precept of the Church. Neither has gone quite to the bottom of the subject. Remaining on the surface, they could only see that celibacy had for basis some intrinsic reason independent of a political one, the holiness inseparable from the ecclesiastical ministry. We do not wish to say, however, that celibacy is anything but a matter of discipline, and that the Church can, under certain circumstances, make an exception to the rule. But this discipline has roots so deep, and is so intimately bound up with dogma and with the character of the priesthood, that it is impossible for the Church to abolish it. It has been observed from the dawn of Christianity and under most adverse circumstances. Irrefutable testimony has established this fact."

A Tirade of Abuse.—Now, the last book which attacks the Catholic Priesthood advances no testimony against the rule of celibacy. In a word, it is simply a tirade of abuse from beginning to end. It is not an edifying sight to see a Protestant minister thus bring disgrace upon his own order. The worthy Protestant clergymen with whom we have spoken about it have condemned the book as sensational and immoral. The very style in which it is printed and bound proves it. No decent, honorable controversialist would attempt anything like it. Men of education and intellect would not glance a second time at it. It is intended only to beguile the ignorant and pander to the depraved taste of a small class.

Persons eminent for sanctity, for great learning, of noble lives and purity of purpose, do not go about preaching a crusade of this kind against the Catholic Church. No ignorance is so dense as the ignorance of fanaticism. The bigot is generally, if not always, an illiterate and ill-bred person. To argue with him would be useless.

No Decent Authority Quoted.—The first thing that strikes the reader in this work is the almost total absence of any decent authority to support the extraordinary statements in which it abounds. The favorite and perpetually recurring authorities quoted are apostate priests,—men dismissed from the service of the Church on account of their scandalous lives,—such as Llorente, Hogan (the author of the schism in Philadelphia sixty years ago), and the infamous Father Chiniqui, of more modern times.

Llorente's Bad Career.—Don Juan Antonio Llorente, born at Calatorra, in Spain, 1756, was a traitor alike to his Church and to the State. He was secretary to the Inquisition at Madrid, for two years, from 1790 to 1792, and was dismissed for irregular conduct. Detected in secret correspondence with the enemies of his country, in 1793, on writing letters of repentance he was received again into favor. At the court of Ferdinand VII., King of Spain, he was loaded with honors, and yet, on the first invasion of the French, he turned traitor to his country and ranged himself on the side of her enemies. He now paid his court to the new king, Joseph Bonaparte, taking the oath of fidelity to him; was appointed one of his secret counsellors; and at the command of Joseph he began, in 1809, to write a history of the Spanish Inquisition. When the sun of the Bonaparte family was set forever, he again paid his court to King Ferdinand, whom he had already abandoned and betrayed, addressing letters full of flattery to the king and to the Chapter at Toledo. When his arts proved unavailing, he gave way to all the bitterness of his heart, writing his " Portraits of the Popes," full of invectives and misrepresentations.

He was finally banished from France for improper conduct. When accused of illicit relations with a French countess, at the age of 66, his friends defended him on the ground that he had previously married her, although he was a priest who had vowed celibacy. He finally died at Madrid, February 25th, 1823, in the 67th year of his age. Had the Spanish government and the Inquisition been such as he represented them, he would not, perhaps, have been permitted to re-enter Spain and terminate his life peacefully in his own country. Ranke, an unexceptional Protestant witness, in his " History of the Ottoman and Spanish Empires in the Seventeenth Century," testifies that Llorente wrote the book in the interest of the Josephine administration, adding that "the Inquisition was, in spirit and tendency above all, a political institution." "The Pope," he says, "had an interest in thwarting it, and he did so as often as he could, but the king had an interest in constantly upholding it."

As a sample of Llorente's fairness, it is sufficient to quote a fact which he makes public in his own work, namely, that he destroyed all the reports of that tribunal, with certain exceptions. So that he admits that he burned the documents of that very institution whose history he undertook to write. (Balmez's Protestantism and Catholicity Compared, page 401.)

HOGAN.—The Reverend Mr. Hogan was dismissed from the seminary of Maynooth for irregular conduct; from the diocese of Limerick for irregular conduct; from the diocese of New York for the same cause, and having been solemnly excommunicated from the Catholic Church, he recanted his errors; then fell back again, married and remarried, became a custom house officer in Boston, and then wrote scurrilous pamphlets against the Catholic Church, intended to fill his purse and awaken anti-Catholic and Know-Nothing prejudices. (Shea and de Courcey's History of the Church in the United States, page 231).

And yet, these are the authorities just and potent this minister brings forth as his witnesses in supporting his infamous charges!

On page 20 the apostle of this filthy crusade says:— "That a woman may obey the priest *in everything he commands her to do*, and that she can never be called to account to God for any action which may have been performed to please her priest." We distinctly charge the Reverend author with the grossest ignorance of Catholic doctrine, or the grossest misrepresentation.

We defy him to point out any statement of any Catholic authority that teaches or insinuates the monstrous doctrine that "a women may obey a priest in everything that he commands her to do," and that "God will not call her to account for any action performed to please the priest."

Wholesale Calumny.—In the next sentence, he states that "penitents are compelled to answer questions of the most revolting character," that "every priest is compelled by *his oath* to pollute the minds and the hearts of the mothers, wives, and daughters with whom he comes in contact." What is this unheard of oath? The author does not pretend to advance one word of proof in support of this awful and wholesale calumny.

Another authority quoted by him is Michelet, with regard to whom one may consult Spalding's Miscellanies, Vol. ii., pages 436 to 452.

On page 44, he states that Pope Siricius, (from the year 384 to 398), first enjoined the celibacy of the clergy. In the very document contemplated by the author the Pope goes on to state that the law of celibacy was already an old custom in the Church.

On page 49, the author says that Ambrose led in the fight against celibacy, which is nonsense. Ambrose always held and taught the efficacy of celibacy.

On page 50, he states that a part of the ablest patrons of Romanism held that celibacy was historically false, and gives as authorities Erasmus, Polydorus, Alvarus, and Pius. Polydorus and Alvarus are unknown, Erasmus is no theologian of any reputation as a Catholic, and Pope Pius the Second never said what the author attributes to him.

Dens.—On page 74, according to the author, (*passim*) every priest wallows in the impurities of

Dens. In the first place, not a copy of Dens can be had in any Catholic store in America! Consequently, how are the clergy and students to provide themselves with the volume in question? Secondly, the parts objected to in Dens are simply necessary portions of moral theology, to be read with proper precaution, and not to gratify a prurient mind, but to avoid grave mistakes in serious matters, such as would be the direction of conscience. It can be no worse for the moralist to discuss sins of the soul, as we have already remarked, than for the physician or surgeon to instruct himself with regard to diseases of the body, and one might as well object to improper impressions to be formed from reading medical works as to the scientific treatment of similar subjects in theology. Objections might be plausibly urged even against portions of Scripture.

On page 99 and subsequent pages is a great deal of rubbish, and falsehood, and nonsense, with regard to the *Sacred Order of the Blessed Creatures.* We are quite safe in offering a reward of ten thousand dollars to any-one who can prove the existence of such an order. It is a most astonishing exhibition of the facility with which people can be imposed upon, that they are willing to believe, even for a moment, in the existence of such an association. The man who can believe that such things are practised in the Catholic Church could believe anything.

A Mysterious Institute.—On page 111 the author professes to note the obligations of members joining this wonderful mysterious institute. Thus the candidate "swears implicit obedience to all clergymen, members of the society, especially to him who shall be her pastor," and also to be most faithful in the discharge of all duties, "particularly in not revealing the secrets, insignia, or duties of the society." In answer to this, we affirm that there is no such society in the entire world; consequently, no such oath. Only a simpleton could accept such stories.

Next, he asserts that the candidate states what is the language and conduct of every female member and reports the same; that the candidate promises and swears to take vengeance and to pursue even to death any member who may become dissatisfied with the requirements of the clerical members; to deny, under oath if need be, any charge or statement made against a clergyman that may be reported to the outside world. If she be a married woman, she promises to be faithful to her pastor and to consider and serve him, if a member, as her only true and lawful husband, blessed before God and His Church, and also agrees to abstain from serving her ostensible husband, as the laws of man are more binding than the laws of God. We never read more arrant nonsense and more wicked lies than the foregoing. Other drivel in the same strain, on page 112, we forbear to quote.

STRANGE CREDULITY.—On page 140 the reverend ignoramus says:—" The next day she told me that in the Convent it was imperative to take communion every day, and that it required nearly a whole day." If any one will attend any mass in any Catholic church and see people approach the altar to receive Holy Communion, he will ascertain how much time it takes to receive the sacrament. How can anybody in his senses affirm that an act which takes about half a minute requires nearly a whole day? It is hard to conceive the credulity of Protestants who can be imposed upon by such palpable lies as this.

As to Maria Monk's " awful disclosures," (page 152,

and the following pages), Colonel Stone, of this City, took the trouble to go to Montreal on purpose and to refute her romance. He proves it to be a romance in almost every particular. As a question of veracity between Maria Monk (a bad creature, according to her own account, and who afterwards died as a drunken harlot on Blackwell's Island) [1] and Colonel Stone, a reputable Protestant gentlemen of New York, the choice is not ambiguous.[2]

On page 161 it is stated that the nuns were taught over and over again that the priest could not sin. Whoever taught such nonsense as this? It is bad enough for Protestants to say that Papal infallibility means that the Pope cannot sin, but whoever yet taught that no single one of the two hundred thousand priests of the Catholic Church could not commit sin?

AN AMUSING BLUNDER.—One of the most amusing blunders of this book is the account of the training of the candidates for priesthood. He says the young men give themselves to "the study of ridiculous theology." This man, utterly ignorant of the first principles of theology, presumes to criticise the theology of the Catholic Church, that has produced the greatest thinkers on deep religious questions. He affirms that "every discussion against popery is so severely forbidden that he who reads any such discussions incurs excommunication *ipso facto* ; therefore, the students are unaware of the doctrines of other religions." Where does this person find sanction for such excommunication? Is he inventing a theology of his own? And is he playing Pope, and flinging around anathemas according to his own sweet will?

[1] See Bishop England's Works, Vol. 5, p. 418.
[2] See Bishop England's Works, Vol. 5, pp. 397–398 et seq.

What Catholic ever heard of such excommunication? What Catholic list of censures ever mentions such a ridiculous one as this? Truly, "the theology" of the man "is ridiculous." If he ever dipped into any book of Catholic theology, he would find that the dogmas of other religions are very accurately stated. Consequently, theological students cannot be unaware of the doctrines of other religions, except by their own negligence. But let us enter this wonderful training school of priests. "Impenetrable silence," he says, "is the rule." In what seminary? In what house of learning? Is it a new institution of his own imagination? He says the young ecclesiastics take the vows of celibacy, obedience, and poverty, and in due time learn to break them all. Where does the ecclesiastical student promise to observe the vow of poverty? Is this writer so very ignorant that he does not know the first rudiments of ecclesiastical life?

Let us consider the distribution of time in his seminary? "All arise at 1:30 A. M. and assemble in the choir to sing Latin canticles, known as Matins." Here he confounds all seminarians with an order of monks; and not even all monks arise in the night to sing matins, but only those like the Carthusian monks in France. After meditation, two Masses follow, according to his fertile imagination; then a further meditation. The beds are put in order before breakfast, and after breakfast three-quarters of an hour are again devoted to the necessary household work. What household work, considering that every seminary in the country has a full staff of servants? Then examination of conscience, one-fourth of an hour. This exercise, at that particular time, takes place in no seminary in the world. Afterwards follow Vespers, spiritual reading, and again, at

5:45, each one goes to arrange his room. What has disturbed it during the day? We have, according to this Reverend blunderer, "two hours a day assigned to study; one occupied with Latin grammar, and the other in translating into English a few Latin verses of Scripture."

THE TRUTH STATED.—Now, if any man will take up the Third Plenary Council of Baltimore, page 85 to 90, and see the course made obligatory in all seminaries of the United States, embracing Logic, Metaphysics, Ethics, the principles of Natural Law, natural sciences, Dogmatic and Moral Theology, biblical exegesis, ecclesiastical history, canon law, theoretical and practical liturgy, sacred eloquence, ascetical theology, and consider how all this is narrowed down to " one hour of Latin Grammar and another hour of Latin version;" that, moreover, no one can be admitted into the ecclesiastical seminary unless he has already studied at least six years in a preparatory institution, devoting his time to the classics and the various branches pertaining to a college course, he will wonder more and more at the intolerable impudence and effrontery of the man who, with all these documents staring him in the face, and within the reach of every one, nevertheless dares to put forth to the public such bold and unblushing lies; and yet this is the reverend gentleman who poses as the advocate of truth?

QUESTIONS IN CONFESSION.—On the interrogations or questions to be made in Confesssion we might quote Könings, II. p. 154–II. n. 4. (L. vi. 607. ii.) p. 157, 2), but it is unnecessary.

All theologians admit and teach that it is better confesssion should lack completeness than that scandal arise by imprudent questions. An imprudence of this kind would be committed when it would involve the risk of doing more harm than good, as,—*e.g.*, if the penitent should thereby be led to learn some evil that he did not previously know. The Roman Ritual, on the Rubrics for the Sacrament of Penance, insists particularly on prudence in asking questions in the Sacred Tribunal, lest any one should learn things of which he was hitherto unconscious, and so learn how to commit sin.

AN ILL-EQUIPPED CONTROVERSIALIST. — We will not load this book with further quotations. Any one desirous of still further studying the confessional may consult the best standard Catholic works we have cited. For this man to have discharged his task properly, he ought first to have made an accurate study of Roman Catholic dogmas and practices before passing a sweeping condemnation. Common fairness to a foe demands this. It is clear he has made no such preparation whatever. In the first place he does not quote, at first hand, a single Catholic author. In the second place, his favorite war-horses and his great arsenals are apostate priests and nuns, such as Llorente, Hogan, Maria Monk, Rebecca Theresa Reid, and Chiniqui. The Rev. Dr. Forbes was once a Protestant minister, and then a Catholic, and finally he returned to his first belief. The Rev. Dr. Edward McGlynn is a suspended priest who has time and again spoken slightingly and insultingly of the Pope, and has vigorously denounced what he terms "the ecclesiastical machine." These are men above the ordinary standard and Dr. Forbes' private character was unblemished. Now, if the alleged abominable practices existed, if such a society of women were a fact, would not Dr. Forbes have revealed the practices and denounced the society, and would he not have published that as a valid reason for his abandonment of the Catholic Church? Would not Dr. McGlynn do the same? Is he the kind of a man who would be silent under such circumstances? No, Dr. McGlynn and men like him have condemned all that they can conscientiously condemn in the Catholic system, and that is very little.

PRACTICAL RESULTS A TEST.—A good test of a religious system is its practical results. "A tree is known by its fruits." Christianity, says St. Cyprian, makes men better, chaste, gentle, honest. Now do men improve by leaving the Catholic Church? Are they not weeds thrown by the Pope over his garden wall, such as Maria Monk, Leahy, and Hogan?

Do not the best minds and hearts of Protestantism return to the Catholic Church? The author of the scurrilous work we refer to has called England the stronghold of Protestantism. It was, and he does not know that the stronghold is capitulating. In 1885, W. Gordon Gorman published a little book called "Converts to Rome."

ROME'S RECRUITS.—There a list of nearly 4,000 English Protestants who had gone over to the Catholic Church during the 19th century was printed. There is hardly a single noble family that has not given one or more of its members to the Roman Catholic Church. To mention a few names at random, they are:—

The Duke of Leeds, the Marquis of Bute, the Marquis of Ripon, the Earl of Abingdon, the Earl of Ashburnham, the Earl of Buchan, the Earl of Denbigh, the Earl of Dunraven, the Earl of Gainsborough, the Earl of Granard, the Earl of Orford, Lord Beaumont, Lord Braye, Lord North, grandson of the third Earl of Guilford, Lord Courtenay, of Christ College, Oxford, Lord Alexander Gordon Lennox, Sir George Bowyer,

Bart., D. C. L., of Oxford, Sir Vere Francis de Vere, Sir Charles Wolseley, the Hon. Edward Douglas, of Christ Church, Oxford, the Hon. and Rev. George Spencer, M. A., the Hon. Gilbert Chetwynd Talbot, D. D., of Christ Church, Oxford, Field-Marshal Sir J. Foster Fitzgerald, Arthur à Becket, Gilbert à Becket, Hugh Gladstone, a cousin of the Right Hon. W. E. Gladstone, Edwin Dwyer Gray, M. P., proprietor of the *Dublin Freeman's Journal,* Charles Lister Mivart, brother of Professor St. George Mivart, F. R. S., Mrs. Butler (née Thompson, painter of the "Roll Call") Charles Hallé, the pianist, Wybert Rousby, the actor, Charles Santley, the baritone, General Michael Bruce, of the Coldstream Guards, General Crispin, General Webber, and Major-General Stewart Allen.

Also—Colonel David La Touche Colthurst, M. P., Colonel C. A. Goodfellow, R. E., Admiral George Courtney, Admiral Crispin, Admiral Robert Hall, Admiral Russel, Henry Manners, F. R. S., Captain Granville Wood, R. N., Dr. C. Carter Blake, F. G. S., Dr. Robert Clarke, M. R. C. S., Dr. Fowler, M. R. C. S., John Bridge Aspinall, Q. C., Isaac Butt, Q. C., M. P., J. A. Cook, barrister, Miss Emily Bowles, authoress, Thomas Cooper, journalist and author, James Grant, novelist, R. B. Knowles, son of Sheridan Knowles, John Oxenford, poet, dramatic author, and critic of the London *Times,* Coventry Patmore, the poet, Adelaide Anne Procter, W. Clement Scott, Aubrey de Vere, the poet. Harold Kyrle Bellew, the actor, Rev. George Bampton, Rev. J. C. M. Bellew, the celebrated elocutionist, Dr. Newman, Cardinal Manning, the Duchess of Argyle, the Dowager Duchess of Athole, lady-in-waiting to her majesty the Queen, the Dowager Duchess of Buccleuch, the Duchess of Hamilton, the Duchess of

Newcastle, the Marchioness of Lothian, the Marchioness of Queensbury, the Countess of Clare, the Countess of Kenmare, the Countess of Orford, the Lady Beaumont, the Lady Arundell of Wardour, Lady Evelyne Bertie, Lady Gray, and Lady Sussex Lennox.

In addition there are numbers of the brightest intellects of the universities and a long list of ladies belonging to the first families in the land.

VOICES OF DISTINGUISHED CONVERTS.—And now listen to Monsignor Preston, a convert of the time of Dr. Forbes; writing in the " Forum," of Feb., 1888, he says:—

" I may add only a few words as to my experience of the Catholic Church from my practical knowledge of her. She can be judged justly only from within. I had learned to appreciate and admire the Church from her exterior and the objective proofs of her divine mission. . . . When I entered I found much more than I had ever hoped to find. I found a system so well adapted to my spiritual needs that this experience alone would have convinced me of its divinity. I found the supernatural without any loss of the natural. . . . I found . . . great natural gifts, learning and culture, such as I had not seen before, were all around me. . . Yet in all such souls there was the absence of self-consciousness, and there appeared the attractive fruit of long mental and moral discipline. . . I had lived among Protestants of piety and refinement, but the Catholic Church presented me with a much higher life. . . . The great virtues which I had always admired the most, humility, purity, and charity, were around me like the fruits of the heavenly grace for which my soul thirsted. To say the least, life would have been worth living were it only to see and know that which has been my happy experience."

DR. NEWMAN.— The fame of the Very Rev. Dr. Newman (now Cardinal) has travelled throughout the world. His virtues and his genius are unquestioned. Here is his testimony to the purity of the Catholic hierarchy. In a postscript appended to the fourth edition of his "Letter to the Duke of Norfolk," issued in April, 1875, in answer to a remark of Mr. Gladstone, Dr. Newman wrote:—

"From the day that I became a Catholic to this day, now close upon 30 years, I have never had a moment's misgiving that the Communion of Rome is that Church which the Apostles set up at Pentecost, which alone has the adoption of sons, and the glory, and the covenants, and the revealed law, and the service of God, and the promises, and in which the Anglican Communion, whatever its merits and demerits, whatever the great excellence of individuals in it, has, as such, no part. Nor have I ever for a moment hesitated in my conviction, since 1845, that it was my clear duty to join that Catholic Church, as I did then join it, which in my conscience I felt to be divine. . . . Never for a moment have I wished myself back."

The illustrious Cardinal Manning, another convert, has written in the same strain. Is it conceivable that high-minded, fearless men like the latter and those mentioned before in Mr. Gorman's book, would tolerate for an instant the unspeakable wickedness "universally practised" (according to the ministerial crusader) by Catholics? The silence of these thousands of recruits would be a greater marvel than the atrocities themselves. The monstrous credulity of the author himself is appalling; his story of the "Blessed Creatures" and ecclesiastical seminaries can come only from a diseased brain.

GARBLED EXTRACTS.—His failure to verify citations

is equally remarkable. He attempts to quote St. Alphonsus Liguori, but garbles his meaning in every case, for instance, with regard to hearing Mass on Sundays. to the petty thefts of servants, to cursing and swearing, and occasions of sin. If he could only have the grace to study a text-book of moral theology—such as Lemkuhl, Sabetti, or Gury—he would be filled with admiration at the consummate learning, the zeal for souls, the prudence and wisdom displayed throughout.

If the laws of the Church and the exhortations of theologians be observed nothing can be conceived more conducive to spiritual progress than sacramental confession. Let the reader consult Sabetti, p. 646, and Gury II., page 276.

IN CATHOLIC DAYS.—The Rev. Father Balmez, in comparing the effects of Protestantism and Catholicity on the civilization of Europe, says:—

"Where Christianity has not existed the people have been the victims of a small number, whose disdains and insults have been the only recompense of their labors. . . . . Observe the grand phases of European society at the time when Catholicism exclusively predominated. With various forms, distinct origins, different inclinations, they all follow the same course; all tend to favor the cause of the multitude; whatever has this for its aim endures: whatever has not, perishes. Whence comes it that this was not the case in other countries? . . . . Let those who represent Catholicism as the enemy of the people point out to us a single doctrine of the Church sanctioning the abuses under which the people were suffering, or the injustice which oppressed them. Let them show us whether, at the commencement of the 16th century, when Europe was under the exclusive domination of the Catholic religion, the people were not as far advanced as they could be, considering the ordinary course of things."

No one has yet taken up that challenge to come out victorious.

# CHAPTER XIV.

## Ministers Who have Erred.

"LOOK ON THIS PICTURE AND ON THIS"—A PARTIAL LIST OF PROTESTANT CLERGYMAN WHO HAVE GIVEN SCANDAL—AN ARGUMENT FOR CLERICAL CELIBACY—BROKEN MARRIAGE VOWS.

We must preface this chapter with the remark that the *tu quoque* argument is always an undesirable one. We are not aware that any Catholic writer has resorted to it, and as a matter of fact it is condemned by fair controversialists. The golden rule in the Church is "charity towards all, malice towards none."

In introducing the *tu quoque* argument here, therefore, we claim to be original. We do not think it fair, however, that a certain class of our opponents should be allowed to iterate and reiterate the charge that the Catholic Church has had some bad priests, without being gently reminded that a great deal more can be said against their own side. In the strange book which we have referred to in the preceding chapter mention is made of one or two priests who have sinned. If that writer's researches could have enabled him to adduce more "terrible examples," he would cheerfully have given them, without doubt. We do not claim that every priest is perfect—and is it not bad logic to argue that, because one or two apples on a tree are rotten, therefore the whole tree is rotten?

Our acquaintance with Protestant clergymen in different parts of the world has instilled respect for them as a body. We are not fanatical. We gladly pay our tribute of admiration to an order which possesses so many noble, virtuous, learned men. And some of the noblest, the most virtuous, the most learned, have finally embraced the Catholic religion. We would not for a moment insinuate that, because there are ministers who have grievously sinned, a body which has given to the world good citizens, good husbands, good fathers, should be sweepingly condemned.

No, our purpose is to show that clerical celibacy is more conducive to virtue than the married priesthood, and that in the latter state there are to be found a greater number of backsliders than in the former. The instances we give below clearly prove that there is more danger in a married ministry than in a celibate priesthood, and that the commission of sin in the former creates a great scandal. Another notable fact—we have not gone outside of America for examples. If we gave instances from other Protestant countries the list would be interminable. Moreover, we have confined ourselves to the last few years.

In January, 1888, great scandal was given by the fall of Bishop B——, of the town of L——, ten miles from L——, Pa. A daily paper said:—

"An old man, honored by the Christian denomination of which he was a member with the highest office in its gift, and known hitherto as one whose life exemplified his pulpit teachings, has confessed a sin that made necessary his deposition from the office of clergyman and bishop. Rev. C—— B——, seventy years old, many years identified with the Church, and for a generation at least one of the most venerated residents of the town of L——, stands before the community self-convicted of immorality. One redeeming feature in the sad affair is that the name of the unfortunate woman involved is kept out of the reach of those who revel in scandal. The ex-Bishop inherited his clerical office almost. For generations the family of which he is a member has been prominent in the Church. He himself was a student of the Scriptures, apparently an earnest worker for the Christianizing of his fellow men, and since 1860 a Bishop. His father and grandfather were ministers. His fall is the sensation of the day in this region. Mr. B——'s fellow laborers in the Church desired to deal with him without harshness. His honored ancestry, his own services in the Church's behalf were remembered. But the cause of religion in general, the good repute of the denomination in general, left them but one resource. They deposed him from his clerical position and excommunicated him from fellowship."

In 1887 and 1888 the whole country was talking of the doings of the Rev. G—— S——, of Minn. On Feb. 15, 1888, the following appeared in almost every journal of the country:—

"The story of the elopement of Rev. G—— S——, the pastor of the Methodist church here, with Mrs.—— the wife of the editor of——, their flight to Europe, their pursuit by the irate scribe, their capture and pathetic parting in New York City, is still a matter of much interest here. For several months Mrs. —— has been in retirement, unwilling to receive the visits even of professed friends, and has never appeared upon the streets of J——. Since her divorce she has been living with her parents, who now keep her more secluded than ever. The divorced husband is still keeping his eyes on the movements of Mr. S——. Hearing that he was in

G——, Mich., H—— prepared a handbill and dropped 300 copies around him there. The citizens of G—— made the place to hot to hold S——, and he departed to Illinois, where he met his wife and family and united with them again. Finding this out, Mr. H—— printed S——'s picture and a vigorous denunciation on the reverse side of the G—— handbills, and flooded that part of the State with the new edition, of which he exultantly avows the authorship. It denounces S—— as a hypocrite, 'snivelling about the Saviour to attract the attention of women and to ruin them.' It relates S——'s J—— experiences, charging him with whipping and attempting to poison his wife and embezzling the missionary funds of the church there. H—— intimates his intention to follow S—— up wherever he goes.

The Rev. C. F. B——, Pastor of the Methodist Episcopal Church in M——, N. J., was charged with criminally assaulting Miss. K—— L——, the daughter of a well-to-do farmer in P——, where B—— once resided, on the 10th of January, 1880. The trial, which took place on the 11th of January, 1880, developed a rather sensational episode.

The Rev. W—— T. E——, Pastor of the Methodist Episcopal Church in B——, N. J., was charged with taking liberties with some lady members of his congregation, on March 24th, 1880. He pleaded guilty to the charges, and his resignation was accepted.

The Rev. H. G. H——, Pastor of the German Lutheran Evangelical Church in W—— H——, was charged with adultery, on February 2d, 1880. He pleaded guilty to the charges, and his resignation was accepted.

The Rev. J. N. S——, Pastors of the Presbyterian Church, G——, was tried and found guilty of criminal relations with Miss L. P——, on January 12th, 1879. Miss

P—— was formerly a Sunday School teacher in his church and at the trial appeared against him. After being tried and found guilty, Pastor S—— quitted the County.

The Rev. W—— P——, pastor of the S—— G—— B—— C—— in New York, was tried on January 20th, 1880, on a charge of intimacy with H—— M——. That was the third time the pastor was arraigned, and, strange to say, the charges were pigeon-holed. He was a married man of family, and at the trial his wife appeared against him. On his promise to abstain from such actions in the future, he was allowed to remain in his pastorate!!!!

The Rev. A—— P——, Pastor of S—— G—— Methodist Episcopal Church, H—— Co., Conn., was committed to the M—— County Jail on December 22d, 1879, for 30 days, for lascivious carriage. He was 60 years of age, and a man of family. Some time previous to his arrest, he was preaching in a neighboring town, and while there made improper proposals to a young lady of his congregation. Brooding over this insult her mental troubles made the young lady a raving maniac. At the trial he barely escaped lynching.

The Rev. E. S. F——, Pastor of the U—— Church at N—— A——, Mass., was charged, on November 21st, 1879, with gross, immoral, and licentious conduct, falsehood, misrepresentation, deceit, and conduct unworthy of a Christian Minister. These charges were made to the Committee of Fellowship, Ordination, and Discipline, of the Massachusetts Convention of Universalists.

The Rev. M. T——. Pastor of the M. E. Church in W—— H——, N. J., was charged, on December 24th, 1879, with slandering M—— D—— B——, one of his

Sunday School Teachers. He unsuccessfully tried to become a boarder at the home of Mrs. D—— B——, and after being refused, was a constant visitor at their home, until he made indecent overtures to M——. He was removed from the pastorate.

The Rev. W. W. D——, Pastor of the B—— S—— B—— Church, Boston, was arrested on August 19th, 1880, for intimacy with Mrs. A—— T——. Mrs. T—— was also arrested. The most undeniable proofs of their guilt existed. Mrs. T——'s husband, with a few more friends, found Mrs. T—— and Pastor D—— undressed in Mrs. T——'s room. He was tried, found guilty, and suspended from his pastorate.

Bishop S——, of Episcopal Diocese of N——, was charged, on April 8th, 1880, with familiar intercourse with one of his domestics named "G——." Before coming to N——, he resided in P——' and after vacating his pastoral residence in the latter place the dead body of an infant was found in the ice house. The Coroner was summoned, and A—— S——, another domestic in the Bishop's employ, related the following story:—

"The Bishop kept three girls, one of whom was called 'G——.' We all knew that he was intimate with G——, and I informed the bishop's wife, but all to no purpose. Months wore on and finally Bishop S—— sent G—— away, and told the remaining portion of his household that 'She got a new place.' But she returned again, after a lapse of three weeks, and informed me that her baby was born, adding that Bishop S—— was the father of it."

The Rev. G—— B——, of B——, was tried, on March 6th, 1886, for slandering and annoying the wife of Judge A. A. P——. Mrs. P—— swore that B——

made her numerous improper proposals, followed her to the watering places and on the streets, vainly trying to cajole her into surrendering her virtue. He also forged letters purporting to be written by her, which he threatened to make public, if Mrs. P—— should expose his guilt.

The Rev. A. D. S——, Pastor of St. L——'s Episcopal Church, B——. was prohibited from preaching or exercising any ministerial functions, on January 24th, 1886. He was previously in charge of a pastorate at H——, N. S., and while there contracted a large amount of debts. Hence his suspension. The Bishop at H—— telegraphed the B—— clerical authorities to suspend S——, adding that he spent the greater part of his H—— salary in buying presents for the ladies. Pastor S—— declined to pay the bills and returned to his home in England.

The Rev. J. D. L——, Pastor of the Methodist Episcopal Church, W——. N. Y., was charged, on January 14th, 1880, with "unministerial conduct, and immoral practices" towards some lady members of his congregation. He was a married man and had four children, but always displayed a strong liking for "kissing the ladies." He was tried by a conference of Methodist clergymen, and Mrs. E—— C——, Mrs. B. H. W——, and Miss C—— W——appeared against him. They swore that Pastor L—— often followed them to their homes and kissed them by force.

The Rev. H—— A. C——, Pastor of the Methodist Episcopal Church at T——, near S——, N. Y., was charged, on January 13th, 1880, with intimacy with a young girl named McC——. The trial had to be abandoned, as the Pastor's friends claimed he was hopelessly insane. His intimacy with Miss McC—— continued over one year.

The Rev. V―― W――, Pastor of the "Bethlehem Mission" in W――, B――, N. Y., was charged with undue intimacy with the wife of H―― S――, a well known B―― merchant, on December 24th, 1880.

Among other cases in which ministers have given scandal in their Church, are the following:—

At 3 o'clock, on May 9th, 1880, the northern Presbytery of New York passed a resolution suspending the Rev. N―― W―― from his functions until he showed contrition and submission. The charges preferred against him were: 1st, That in public and private he bade defiance to the Presbytery; 2d, That he was guilty of a violation of the good order of the House of God in P――, where he wanted to preach without being called or invited to preach there; 3d, That he published a book, styled "Vindication," which threw scandal on the Church.

The Rev. A. W. J――, Pastor of the B―― M. E. Church, T――, S. I., was tried, on December 31st, 1878, for misappropriating funds belonging to the church of which he was also treasurer. The board of trustees gave him $300 to pay Mr. J.――W―― an account of a mortgage due on the church. Instead of paying Mr. W――, the Pastor converted the church funds to his own use. He was removed from the pastorate.

The following was telegraphed to various newspapers from W――, P-, under date of Jan. 21st, 1881:—

"About six months ago the Rev. J―― J. B―― of P――accepted a call to the Presbyterian church in F――, this country. The many social qualities of the young minister soon made him a universal favorite with the members of his congregation, particularly the female portion, who thought there was no preacher so nice as Mr. B――. Many church festivals were held, and the pastor was the centre of attraction at all times and upon all occasions. After awhile it began to leak out that Mr. B—— was neglecting his pastoral labors and paying too much attention to the female portion of the flock. These rumors, however, could not be substantiated at that time, and the elders refused to take any action, which they were urged to do by several members.

Rev. S—— M. S——, of E—— L—— and St. G—— N. Y., W——, O., married—Assault with intent to murder his wife, shot his wife, then himself, adultery with one of his congregation.

Rev. R. S——, of M——V——, Ind., married—Adultery, betrayed and eloped with girl of 17, deserted wife and children, embezzlement of Church funds (1878.)

Rev. J. M. S——, of A——, I—— immoralities with little girls at his asylum school, assault on 8 year old girl, none of the girls more than 15 (1876).

Rev. C. T——, of I—— and B——, Wis., married girl—only 15 years old.

Rev. A——T——, of E——, Ill., and N——Y.—— married—Adultery, seduced Mrs. C——, robbed her, deserted his wife, said in court, " We all do such things, more or less ;" 5 years in Sing Sing (1881).

A Catholic priest would not be allowed to dabble in stock gambling. There is no such restriction upon a Protestant minister. Although the minister in the following case was guilty of no crime, yet his conduct is not edifying in a minister of the Gospel, who should keep clear of stock brokers. The following report was in all the New York papers of Jan. 14th, 1888 :—

"The Rev. C——H——, of J——C——, who is said to have lost largely in speculation through the firm with which Broker S——, who recently failed, was connected, has brought suit to restrain the Stock Exchange from using the proceeds of the sale of S——'s seat (which brought $18,000) from paying out the money.

"In his complaint Mr. H—— alleges that on January 3d he obtained a judgment against S—— for $29, 904.15, an execution being issued on that day. It was not satisfied, because S—— lived in J——C—— and had no property in N—— Y——. Mr. H—— avers that on December 29th, 1887, when S—— failed, he asked the Committee on Admissions to sell his seat, and that it was sold.

"Mr. H—— claims that all of S——'s Stock Exchange debts do not amount to over $12.000, that his seat in the Exchange was worth $20,000, and that the claims of the persons who are made defendants in the suit did not arise from transactions in or through the Exchange, but, as he is informed and believes, are claims 'for money borrowed by S—— and loaned to him by those outside the Exchange, and in no way connected with it.'

"The plaintiff asks that a receiver be appointed; that the defendants be made to account for all of his property received by any of them for the sale of his seat, and that plaintiff's costs and disbursements be paid in preference to those of the defendants."

## CASES SUMMARIZED.

We could easily fill another work, nay several works, with examples similar to the above. We cannot afford to do more than summarize a few :—

The Rev. E ——, K. A——, a married man, of T—— and B—— R. I., Mass., and Ohio—adultery, (1878).

Rev Mr. A——, a married man of Cincinnati, O.—Adultery and drunkenness (1878).

Rev. J. S. A—— (alias J. S. C——), of W—— and C—— City, Iowa, married—Adultery; betrayed the wife of D. C. H——, eloped, deserted wife and children (1880).

Rev. M—— E. A——, of F—— and R——, Iowa—Adultery, betrayed Mrs. K—— N—— (1881).

Rev. T—— B. B——, of P——, married—Adultery, betrayed L—— Y——, a deacon's daughter (1876).

Rev. W. B. B——, of H—— Mo., married—Adultery, betrayal, (1876).

Rev. W. B. B——, of V——, Ky.—assault on girl ten years old, expelled from the Church (1878).

Rev. M—— B——, of F——, Mich.—assault on A—— F——, ten years old (1878).

Rev. W. H. B——, of New York City—assault on young woman of his congregation, resigned (1878).

Rev. Professor W—— F. B——, of I——, Ind., and St. L——, Mo.—Betrayal of Miss C—— E. V—— (was President of College) (1878.)

Rev. M. B——, of B——, E. D.—Adultery, betrayal of servant girl (1878).

Rev. G—— B——, of C——, N. Y., married—Adultery, elopement with Mr. S——'s wife, deserted his own wife and children, general swindling, over $7000, forgery (1878).

Rev. E. L. B——, of W——, Iowa, and C——M—— R——, and O——, M——., married—Betrayed wife of Mr. P—— and eloped with her, deserting wife and four children, sent to State Prison (1879).

Rev. Mr. C. B——, of J——, Mich., married—Adultery, deserted his wife and eloped with one of his congregation (1880).

Rev. A. B. B——, of L——, Kan., married—Adultery, Bigamy, deserted wife, embezzlement (1880).

Rev. P. H. B——, of B——, N. Y.—assault on two young girls (1876).

## Ministers who have Erred.

Rev. T—— B——, of various churches in I——, came from L——, England, married—Adultery,. betrayed L—— C——, deserted wife and children, charged with inhuman cruelty to wife and children (1881).

Rev. Mr. B——, of S—— County, Mo., married—adultery, betrayal of——, 13 years old (1882).

Rev. W. S. C——, of H——, Ill., married—Adultery, with females of deacon's family (1877).

Rev. J. M. C——, of L——, Mass., married—Bigamy (1878).

Rev. S—— C. C——, of St L——, Mo.—assault on Miss C—— C——, 13 years old, and on other girls (1878).

Rev. E. L C—— Bigamy, forgery, swindling (1878).

Rev. A—— C——, of J——, Iowa, 70 years old—assault on A—— A. C——, 13 years old, adultery (1878).

Rev. C—— T. C——, of C——, Va.—assault on I—— T——, 12 years old, assault on other girls (1880).

Rev. T. H. C——, of F—— and St. J——'s, Mich., married—Adultery, betrayal of Miss F—— C—— G—— (1880).

Rev. D—— C——, of H—— and S——, N. Y., married—Adultery, betrayal of A—— O——, servant girl (1881).

Rev. H—— C——, of—— T, N. Y., married, 70 years old—betrayal of a girl 11 years old (1879).

Rev. G. M. D——, of L——, Ill., married—Adultery, with Mrs. W. M. D——, discovered by his wife in church (1882).

Rev. Mr. D——, of Y—— City, Ill., married—Adultery with three of his congregation (1878).

Rev. Mr. D——, of J—— County, Wis., 63 years old—assault on ——, adultery with others, sentence 6 years prison (1878).

Rev. L—— D——, of K——, married—Adultery, deserted wife and eloped with another minister's daughter (1878).

Rev. P—— D——, of N—— Y—— City, married—Deserted wife and family, adultery, eloped with one of his congregation, Miss M—— (1878).

Rev. Dr. J A——. D——, of N—— A——, Ind., and M——, Tenn., married—Adultery, betrayal of Miss L—— K——, attempted suicide, deserted wife and children (1879).

Rev. Wm. D——, of Y—— and T——, N. Y., married—Bigamy and adultery, deceived second wife by telling her his first wife was dead (1881).

Rev. J. B. D——, of P——, married—Adultery, betrayal of one of congregation, immoral assaults on women (1882).

Rev. J—— E——. of P——. Ill., married—with two daughters and daughters-in law, adultery, and —— (1878).

Rev. E—— H. E——, of various churches in M—— and M——, married—Adultery with married women of congregation, arrested in pulpit while preaching (1882.)

Rev. J. H. F——, of H——, Mo., married——Adultery, bigamy, had several wives, gambling (1879).

Rev. Wm. P. F——, of I—— and P——, N. Y.,—Betrayal of Miss C—— W——, adultery (1879).

Rev. I. D. F——, of B——, N. J.—Immoral assault on wife of A. H—— (1880).

Rev. M. F——, of M—— and C——, Ill.—Tried to assault Miss M—— S——, committed assaults on several women (1882).

Rev. J. S. G——, of J—— C——, N. J., and H——, Ill.— Betrayal of a young sister, who committed suicide (1876).

Rev. W. M. G——, of N——, Ind.—C——assault on a little girl (1880).

Rev. C. E. G——, of A—— and B——, Tex., married—Deserted wife and children, adultery, tried to commit bigamy, charged with larceny (1882).

Rev. H—— A. H——, of M——, Ill., married—Deserted wife and family, and committed adultery many times (1878).

Rev. J. H— -, of L—— and G——, Iowa—Adultery, betrayed Miss E—— R—— ; J—— B——, to whom she was betrothed, killed her, and then committed suicide, dying with her in his arms (1878).

Rev. H. R. H——, of L- G—— and D——, Ore.—Adultery with Mrs. A. C. H—— (1879).

Rev. H—— H——, of H——, N. J.—Familiarities with his servant girl, assaulted another woman (1880).

Rev. C. R. H——, of H——, N. J., married—Deserted wife and children, adultery, eloped with one of his congregation, Miss A—— (1880).

Rev. H—— E. H——, of B—— and W——, N. Y., married—, ——crimes, gross immorality with his ——, 11 years old (1880).

Rev. F—— M——, of F——, Md., married—Attempt to commit bigamy, deserting wife and children (1882).

Rev. L. D. P——, of C——, Ky., married—Deserted wife and children, adultery, betrayed and eloped with daughter of Rev. S. S——(1876).

Rev. H. H. H——, of N—— M——, Conn.—Betrayed and then murdered Miss M—— E. S——(1878).

Rev. J—— A. H——, of M—— A——, O.—Bigamy, had three wives (1878).

Rev. A—— H——, of V——, married—Adultery, —— with his ——(1878).

Rev. J—— E. H——, of St. L——, Mo., and R——,

Mass., married—Bigamy, breach of promise, adultery, engaged to marry five of his congregation (1881).

Rev. Mr. H——, of R——, Va.—Murder, adultery, betrayed a young woman of his congregation, killed her to hide his crime (1882).

Rev. C—— H——, of R——, Conn., married—Deserted sick wife and children, cruelty to wife, embezzled church funds, adultery, eloped with married woman of his congregation (1882).

Rev. C. A. K——, of C——, Ga.—Adulteries, betrayed a girl 13 years old in church (1876).

Rev. C. S. K——, of B—— C——, Ida.—, ——, adultery, betrayed niece, Mrs. H—— A. P——(1881).

Rev. Mr. K——, of L——, Pa., married—Adultery, betrayed, eloped with Miss C—— M——, embezzled church funds, deserted wife and children (1882).

Rev. A. H. K ——, of M—— Ind., married—Adultery, attempted to poison wife (1882).

Rev. Mr. L——, of W——, W. Va.—Attempt to —— assault a twelve year old girl (1882).

Rev. J—— L——, of A——, Pa.—Adultery, —— assault on I— Miller, 13 years old (1882).

Rev. S—. H. M-G——, of A——, Ill., married—Adultery with Mrs. L—— P——, murdered his wife, 14 years in State Prison (1877).

Bishop S——M-C——, of D ——, Mich., 75 years old ——, ——, —— long continued with Miss F—— R——, 14 years old, deposed by the House of Bishops (1878).

Rev. H—— C. M——, of G——, N. Y., and St. L—— County, N. Y., married—Adultery, betrayal of M——. B. F——, an invalid, had child, fled while under arrest, escape from justice, deserted wife and children, represented himself as unmarried and engaged to marry respectable lady (1878).

Rev. J——— H. M———, of P———., Pa., and S ———A———. Tex.. married—Adultery for a year, assault on M——— R———. caught by wife (1878).

Rev. J——— M ———, of B———, O.—Bigamy, seven wives (1879).

Rev. S. S. M———, of B———, Pa.—Adultery, betrayal, child by ——— ——— ——— (1879).

Rev. W. R. M——— N———, of P———, G——— County, Md., married—Deserted wife and children, adultery, betrayal of young woman of congregation (1879).

Rev. G. F. M———, of various churches in I——— and M———. Swindling, obtaining money under false pretences, adultery, repeated many times in each place, seduced six married women, drunkenness, lying, profanity, eloped with married woman (1881).

Bishop O———, of N——— Y———, Adultery (1878).

Bishop O ———, of N———J———, Adultery (1878).

Rev. Dr. J. D. F———, of B———. Charged with libel upon Rev. T. B. C———, sued for $40,000; also charged with fighting ; has written a book against Catholic Priesthood (1882).

This person's partial list contains, from 1876 to 1883, 2053 crimes charged against clergymen ; of this number no less than 1113 are crimes against women. An analysis of the list shows that, out of 870 erring clergymen, only 66 are Catholic priests, and of these 66 but 46 have been unchaste.

After this we think our adversaries will see how grossly the Catholic preist has been slandered and how much may be said against the minister.

www.ingramcontent.com/pod-product-compliance
Lightning Source LLC
Chambersburg PA
CBHW031832230426
43669CB00009B/1317